EDITORIAL

FIONA SAMPSON

This avowedly cosmopolitan issue of the *Review* appears at one of the few junctures when poetry in Britain seems to be attracting the domestic attention it deserves. Poetry is on the front pages of newspapers and among the BBC news headlines. Arts programmes are filled with interviews and discussion. We've even had a BBC "multi-platform season", chiefly featuring performance poetry and historical documentaries. And there's been plenty to talk about. After all, May saw the Laureateship pass from Andrew Motion to Carol Ann Duffy; the Oxford Professorship, also voted on in May, passed briefly from the American critic Christopher Ricks to the poet Ruth Padel.

To put it one way, then, all this attention is merely circumstantial, the result of a conjunction between Oxford's five-year and the Palace's new ten-year cycle. Like astronomical – or astrological – phenomena, it's a rare event, which won't be repeated for a decade. 2019, when it comes around, will throw up an entirely different cast and will be an opportunity for further public discussion of poetry and poetics. We should all relax, therefore, and enjoy this surge in popular coverage for what it is: part of the ebb and flow of current affairs.

On the other hand, much of this coverage (rather like that in recent American political history) seems indistinguishable from the headline with which a (male-edited) *Poetry Review* of the 1980s, to its shame, greeted Carol Ann Duffy's victory in the National Poetry Competition: 'Woman Wins' (73:4). As the *Times Literary Supplement* #5536 puts it rather well, this 'Man Bites Dog' take implies that there is something counterintuitive about a woman's being a fine poet. It's hard to imagine such old-fashioned gender shock in other parts of the democratic world: in the US, for example, where Elizabeth Bishop was appointed Consultant in Poetry to the Library of Congress, the post which has evolved into the American Laureateship, back in 1949. Nor do we, surely, still need to rehearse the old Woolfian 'Shakespeare's sister' argument: that it's extraordinary how many fine women poets have managed to emerge over the centuries, despite wholesale exclusion from even literacy.

Perhaps, then, it behoves us to enjoy the media spot-light while it's on poetry, but also to hope that it could widen to illuminate more of a well-furnished stage. In this centenary year of the Poetry Society, for example, there are also stories to tell about continuing good practice. One of these is the

Review's own centenary, which fell in May, as we went to press, and which we celebrate with our centenary anthology, *A Century of Poetry Review* (Carcanet, October, £14.95, ISBN 978 1 84777 016 5). Read like this, 'Cosmopolis' identifies not only today's internationalism, but the sheer variety of voices and cultures we've published over our first century – and look forward to celebrating in the decades to come.

Our new colophon, a Jack-in the-Green or poet with laurel crown, is taken from an edition of *Il Decamerone di Giovanni Boccaccio*, published in London in 1774.

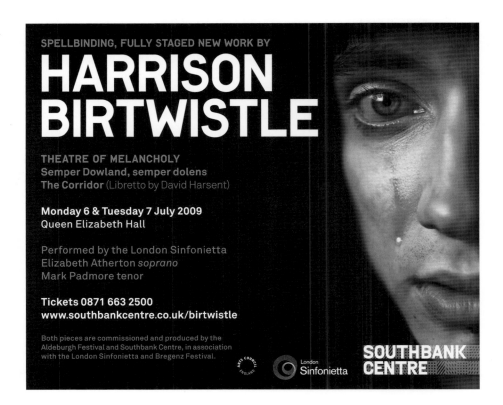

Contents

Volume 99:2 Summer 2009

Editorial

Poems

Centrefold

Reviews

Endpapers

POEMS

Carol Ann Duffy
Cold

It felt so cold, the snowball which wept in my hands,
and when I rolled it along in the snow, it grew
till I could sit on it, looking back at the house,
where it was cold when I woke in my room, the windows
blind with ice, my breath undressing itself on the air.
Cold, too, embracing the torso of snow which I lifted up
in my arms to build a snowman, my toes, burning, cold
in my winter boots; my mother's voice calling me in
from the cold. And her hands were cold from peeling
then dipping potatoes into a bowl, stopping to cup
her daughter's face, a kiss for both cold cheeks, my cold nose.
But nothing so cold as the February night I opened the door
in the Chapel of Rest where my mother lay, neither young, nor old,
where my lips, returning her kiss to her brow, knew the meaning of cold.

Tadeusz Dąbrowski

God has not retired – as Simone Weil
would have it – a huge distance away, but He's
right here, so close that I can feel His

caring non-presence. (Which is a word passed over
in silence, an aborted gesture, a suspended
gaze,
        a breath held for a moment. That
not breathing, that's your life.)

Translated by Antonia Lloyd-Jones

D. Nurkse
Early Morning, Late Summer, Unmade Bed

Remember the suffering of this pronoun *I*,
how this vowel was slighted and betrayed,
how this letter undressed and lay awake
until dawn, when even the bluish elms
were over-burdened with the Self,
even the mirror, window, wineglass

were inhabited by a glint, a radiant edge.
Then she knelt at the head of the bed
to unzip her boot, fork and spoon were reconciled,
this letter was lost in a heaven that hurt
like the labyrinthine labor of the racing mind.
Take your sharp pencil, love, and erase me
from the top down, leaving a smudge
to darken between the naked sleepers.

Jo Shapcott
Viral Landscape

Before I was bounded; now I've begun to leak...
— Helen Chadwick

I went outside looking and looking
for a garden and the hill. I have lost
my shadow and my oak and my night sweat.
The field was just mown and the summer

so hot there was no green in it,
layers of russets and yellows,
and I was swelling with mosquito
bites and I was listening to Fado.

The trees around the perimeter
were a block of solid colour,
shockingly uni-green by contrast.
(my stomach fluttered at the sight – and

gut epithelium is five days old at most)
Look further into the stands of trees
and everything changes (my cerebral
and visual cortex is as old as me). The eye

can't locate an individual shade:
it's all delicate tips and hints
of green rolling in the wind.
We are moving and I can't see a thing.

Procedure

This tea, this cup of tea, made of leaves,
made of the leaves of herbs and absolute

almond blossom, this tea, is the interpreter
of almond, liquid touchstone which lets us
scent its true taste at last and with a bump,

in my case, takes me back to the yellow time
of blood tests, and cellular madness,
and my presence required on the slab

for the surgery, and all that mess
I don't want to comb through here because
it seems, honestly, a trifle now that steam

and scent and steep and infusion say thank you
thank you thank you for the then and now

Atar Hadari
Coat Buying

I dreamed that you and I were in a store
and looking into a long mirror
I had some kind of rucksack on
and was struggling to make a decision;
you thought I should buy this full length coat,
it had patches of red that were oblong,
I think the colour swatches were line ends,
it was the sort of coat you wear when you are still young;
you were wearing black and your glasses were as always formal –
I don't believe you wore a hat
but you stood beside me looking funereal
and I chose not to buy the coat
though all the rest of that night
I was struggling to find my way back
to that coat and trying to change my mind
the way they say you never regret
what you do, only what you don't do –
I woke with the memory of you
saying "Do it" and me saving money
and the small brown notes float over the waves
turning into small orange buoys
for a frog to climb on or a porpoise
and I think that you and I
standing in that Filene's basement
were counting the cost of our lives
you in death, me in the fool's colours
and even now you stand at the hospital
and I patrol the streets buying baby clothes
and all you can know for sure is what you wore
as you waited in the corridor
for the doctor to come and give you the green
mask and smoke while you signed and made for the swing doors
and somebody that said your name as you fled
and maybe held your hand before the colours lost their brilliance
and somebody that held the coat
before you went out into the cold.

Penelope Shuttle
Bedtime

Sometimes, in a domestic crisis,
you'd shrug, adopt a joke accent –

> *I'm joost a leetel happy, joost a leetel sad...*

hoping to jog me out of my crankiness,
offering me (as I well knew), a tender heart.

Sometimes I shrugged back, laughed,
but too often rejected your offering.

If by some magic you could be here again,
I'd stick my hand out
through the bars of my cage of scalding tears
to accept your gift.

If you could be here at midnight to say –
Isn't it time we were in bed?
I wouldn't be up half the night,
beloved, wayward with loneliness.

You

Now there's no trace of you anywhere,

and you're no longer interested in me
or that equally-private creature, the moon,

I'm like someone so far behind with her rent
not even her great grandchildren
will be able to settle the debt –

But sometimes your absence hovers
close to me in the form of a hummingbird

whose bright wings beat the rain into so many rainbows
I'm like the river drinking from her own cupped hands...

Fred Beake
Tu Fu's Lamentation In Autumn And Exile

1

Dew like gems hurts and diminishes the maples in the wood.
From the mountains and gorges of Wu the wind is cold.
Waves, which ought to stay in the river, merge with a frantic sky.
Clouds, wind-tossed above the canyons, touch their shadows.
The chrysanthemums have opened twice, tears for what's been.
The boat of my grief stays moored: I shall never reach home.
In each house they measure and cut the clothes for next year
          And up on the hill
The washblocks thump faster than last night, and as harsh.

2

The last sun glimmers on the remote walls of K'uei-chou.
Each night I find the Dipper and gaze towards the seat of power.
It's true when the gibbon shrieks three times all men weep,
But my tears are for this eight month journey to no-where.
In bed and sick I cannot smell the incense by the official portraits.
Just turrets, white against the hills, and no roll calls.
          But look! Moon shines on ivy
And makes flowers among the reeds on the island's shore!

3

First light: the houses of this town are so still.
Too many days at this time I've sat, immersed, by the blue hills.
Two nights ago the fisherboats came back, and moored, bobbing
– Just as the odd swallow, though autumn is bleak, still flitters:
So what am I but a source of good advice that was ignored,
A reformer of universities, who never made Vice Chancellor.
And yet the friends I went to school with, mainly did well,
And do as they ought to, having swallowed the official pill.

4

Yes, Ch'ang-an has some resemblance to a chessboard,
Which is to remember the bad news of a hundred years.
New pieces to each square, new princes and new nobles:
Gone, the old kind; a new type assumes the official robes.
Always the thump of gongs and drums in the northern passes.
And as on wings, the messengers hurtle to the Army of the West.
And the river of autumn is so cold, and fish and dragon dormant.
My country as it was before these problems never leaves my thoughts!

5

The gatehouse of the Immortals' Palace faces south:
The statues in the river mists have moisture on their lips.
In the west, watch – the mother of the Lord of Gods descends
while from the eastern pass purple haze advances.
And the clouds fold back, and there are screens with rural scenes about a throne
And sun on dragon scales and robes: this is what Heaven looks like!
Once I lay by the river of time to be, and thought of the years to come,
And once I answered an Emperor's summons through a patterned door.

6

From the maw of Ch'ut-tang Gorges to Crooked River
Mist and a slight breeze, and an autumn that will not end.
From Calyx Hill by walled ways imperial processions rolling,
But at Hibiscus Park news from the frontier!
Blinds of pearl, well-made pillars, contained the yellow birds,
And cable and masts kept off the white wild gulls.
        Think of the sound of that music, and mourn!
This, from the first times, was the seat of emperors!

7

In the time of the Han they constructed K'un-ming Pool as a memorial,
And the imperial banners of Wu still waver before my eyes!
But under the moon the weaver girl no longer weaves
And the scales of the great stone whale clatter about in the breeze.
The waves toss up a seed over clouds that seem sunk in the lake,
And the red lotus has dropped its pollen, and has a cold calyx.
      The sky road is only for birds
And by each lake and river the fisher of mortality.

8

By Yu-su river the road to K'un-wu wanders, wanders;
And into Lake Mei-p'i the shadow of Turret Peak falls.
Parrots drop pecked seeds from the scented rice-stalk.
The phoenix perched on the wu-t'ung branch when it grew old.
Lovely girls gathered kingfisher feathers in the Spring:
Immortals in a boat we departed again at evening.
      This brush once coloured the world!
Overwhelmed by words, and looking at things, my head hangs in anguish!

Wendy Cope
From The Audience

Poems commissioned by the Endellion String Quartet

The Radical

I've little patience with this kind of thing –
This trite, post-modern, easy-listening.
I hoped for something far more challenging.
This isn't avant-garde enough.
It really isn't hard enough.
It isn't avant-garde enough for me.

The point is not to please the bourgeois ear.
The good composer is a pioneer
Whose music very few will want to hear.
This isn't cutting edge enough.
It isn't off-the-ledge enough.
It isn't cutting edge enough for me.

Art should disturb. It's not to make us glad.
It isn't to console us when we're sad.
It's to remind us that the world is bad.
This isn't agonised enough.
You're not antagonised enough.
It isn't agonised enough for me.

Repeat ad lib: It really isn't hard enough
              It isn't avant-garde enough *etc.*

The Traditionalist

I like a good tune with a regular beat
From the days before music went wrong –
An old-fashioned melody, catchy and sweet.
I like a good tune with a regular beat.
These modern composers, they can't write a song.
They don't get you tapping your feet.
I like a good tune with a regular beat
From the days before music went wrong.

The Cougher

There's a tickle in your throat
And you've hardly heard a note
And you're wishing you were in some other place.
In this silent, listening crowd
You're the one who'll cough out loud,
And you know you're facing imminent disgrace.

Yes, right now you're in a pickle.
The unmanageable tickle
Is a torment, and it's threatening your poise.
Can you hold out any longer
As the urge to cough grows stronger?
Any moment you'll emit a mighty noise.

If this bloody piece were shorter,
If you had a glass of water,
It would help. But there is nothing you can do.
Oh, if only you could be
Safe at home with a CD,
In an armchair, free to cough the whole way through.

Do you hear a rallentando?
Does this mean the end's at hand? Oh,
What a mercy. Yes, they're really signing off.
They perform the closing bars
And you thank your lucky stars
And it's over. You have made it. You may cough.

Poems commissioned by the Endellion String Quartet to celebrate their 30th anniversary in association with the Norfolk and Norwich Festival, St. Magnus Festival and Cambridge Festival, with additional financial support from Bryan Foster, the Scottish Arts Council and Ralph Vaughan Williams Trust.

David Morley
Camargues

I will wake up in a world that hooves have led to
— Les Murray

Some horses are caves; you catch
that by the way they flicker and shy
at shadow. You can walk inside horses
and sense their walls trembling around you.
Camargues are air-delvers, the pile-driver
we're gripping on our reins, chiselling
granite miles. We caught their backs like luck
then held on. Camargues are not cave,
but they passed through like wraiths
slamming silently through the walls.

Thug-faced, hog-necked, anvil-hoofed
Camargues — necking the paint's hay
on cave walls of Niaux and Lascaux;
cantering behind the wasted warriors
of Rome, Persia and Greece. We rode
them here — or they rode us, chests thumped
out like wagons heaving our wagons;
warmed to our genius grandfathers
because they whispered to them
in horse and only in horse.

We should as well cremate ourselves
alongside our Camargues, riding them
through heaven's walls, hoofed pyres
to our Saints Mary Jacobe and Mary Salome.
We might have fired our horses
on our deaths as we fired our houses;
burnt ourselves upon the deaths
of our horses since we were their houses.
All horses are spells, but Camargues
are myth. You catch that on horseback.

A.A. Marcoff
Composition

the cool & swerve of the shore,
more marvellous than dream:
Leviathan heads off into
blue space – vast symphony
of sea: we are walking
at dawn watching the sun
rise from water as light
penetrates every aspect of our world
with visibility: dawn
comes like a wave: this is
the sea of light & dream,
sea of salt & tongue & sun:
the waters are massive & unearthly,
as horizons curve into the distance
like blue myth: the white flight
of seabirds is hieratic,
a prophecy of light & sky:
waves come & go
like thoughts we surf
in the imagination of the spray:
inner light, a mind of sea...

look, the sun is rising in this sky –
a revelation, & the waves of the sea move
with light: we are celebrants
of the waves & the white chorus of the birds:
we walk into morning poised
on shifting sands, with footprints
for a moment becoming sea
in time, in the cool & swerve
of the beautiful shore, this dream
everlasting... imbued with the deep
blue dawn of God & bird

Arthur Boyars

Adam, Eve And The Serpent, By Lucas Cranach

She offers him the fruit, and he's unsure
Whether to accept or not;

The animals also give him no help,
They cannot tell how this will end;

Only the Serpent knows, since he has hatched the plot,
Relying, as he does, on Man's misconduct,

Slithering down the laden but benighted tree
Unseen by the protagonists –

She, calm and neutral, and he so lost in thought;
We've lived to know the outcome: it was meant for us!

Siriol Troup
Translating Proust

'Longtemps, je me suis couché de bonne heure.'

Thirty pages to describe how he tossed and turned in bed before he
                                              fell asleep,
the hours stretching from *long* to *temps* like smoke from the snuffed
                                              candle,
the match struck at midnight in a lost hotel. Lights out early, the
                                              sound of minutes
scratched away in the room downstairs: creaking woodwork, the
                                              shifting
darkness of tables and oil lamps, rumours of gold under the door.

A lifetime's habits dusted off on the fresh cheeks of his pillow,
the past and its countries flashed back by spinning walls and
                                              stiffened limbs,
whispers of muslin along the hall. High ceilings, insolent clocks, the
                                              pitiless mirror,
the window over the street – all there in that first word, conspiring
                                              with memory
to resist translation.

Tsvetanka Elenkova
Pain

When you hold a bottle and hear the wind
through the open throat
when you put a conch to your ear
the echo pain from the emptied body
and when a single slight hiss
as of a punctured bicycle tyre
finally fills the empty space
like a newborn's wail
Take it carefully in your arms
and give it or don't to its mother
but take it carefully
it's so fragile all cartilage
Give it water or leave it on the shelf
by your head

Translated by Jonathan Dunne

Julian Stannard
Bar Degli Specchi

What I want now is a little Vivaldi
which is terribly *infra dig* in some quarters
but sitting here in The Bar Of Mirrors
where I have been sitting for twenty-five years
drinking a pale version of Green Tea
which is delicately fused with ceramic blue
a Vivaldian quick step might do the trick.
It would be so much better than the song
which is coming from the radio which has something
to do with a bell and the exhortation
to ring it and to ring it and failing that
to lie prostrate on the floor and simply shudder.
If Vivaldi is no longer available or too *infra dig*
a little slow jazz or even a little low jazz
would capture the mood of the city
not to mention the mood of this Green-Blue Tea
which is holding up the sweetness of my tart.
And whilst I have been talking to you
distracting you from the drumbeat of the heart
so many things have been happening:
the mirrors are gleaming and the girl with the cloth
has created a new world order
and the boy, quite beautiful, with his *cioccolata calda*
is lowering a brioche into the dark soup...

Wojciech Bonowicz
Celan

Celan shouts again. Again he wakes up
over the ditch filled with mouths.

Celan – the word that became the flesh
of an old man.

The river that flows
with two currents
in one bed.

Translated by Elzbieta Wójcik-Leese

Timothy Allen
The Wooing Of Kiều By Kim

From A new lament for a broken heart (*a reworking of Nguyễn Du's*
Đoạn Trường Tân Thanh *into English*)

People in love are curious creatures
with unfathomable customs.

When Kim returns behind his book-lined walls,
he realises that he is in love with Kiều.
It is her face that he sees before he falls asleep.
It is she who comes to haunt him in his dreams.
Each day apart from her he calls three autumns.

Silk curtains cover up her far windows:
he imagines parting them to find the rose within.
The moon is always waning, the lamp is burning low:
he longs to press his face against her face.
In his room, the air is frosty, copper-cold:
his brushes are dry; his lute strings hang loose.
Bamboo blinds rattle in the wind.
Incense stirs his desire.
The tea tastes dull: it lacks the lick of her lips.

If fate had not meant to bring them together,
then why did she suddenly appear, that night,
with her beauty that can topple city walls,
to tease the very pupils of his eyes?

He returns to the spot where he first met the girl.
It is the turn of a brook, like any other:
lush green grass and clear water.
Sadness hangs on the breeze at dusk.
The reeds sway, as if to mock him.
He can think of nothing else besides her.

He keeps walking, till he reaches her Blue Bridge.

The gate is locked, the wall is high.
He tries to imagine his way in.

For instance, he might write a poem
so seductively persuasive it will be sure to lure her heart,
on the underside of a fallen red leaf,
and he might set that leaf upon a stream
that will carry the poem within those impregnable walls.
Except there is no such stream.

Or he might attach the same poem
to the leg of an accommodating bluebird,
and encourage the bluebird to squeeze through a crack
in the stonework,
and to fly to her with his messages of love.
But unfortunately there is no such crack
and no such bluebird.

A willow tree hangs its silky curtain.
Sitting in its branches, an oriole laughs at him.
All the doors are locked and bolted,
where is she?

He decides to seek a more conventional entrance.
Sauntering nonchalantly about the outer wall,
he finds, round the back, an empty house.
Its owners are away. The property's for rent.

And that is how the student, Kim, becomes Kiều's neighbour.

He brings his books and his lute and settles in.
It offers everything he needs: trees to hide behind, and rocks.
Even the porch says, in gold letters, *Kingfisher View*,
which is lucky for him, since he knows a kingfisher
that he wants to view.
Each day he opens his window, just a fraction,
so that he can peep towards her eastern wall.
But the spring and the grotto are silent.
He does not even glimpse her red shadow.

Two months have come and gone.
One warm afternoon, beyond the wall,
he sees her walk beneath the peach trees.
He puts down his lute and smoothes his gown,
but when he hurries outside, she is gone.
Her perfume hangs on the breeze.

He searches about the place and finds
a golden hairpin in the branch of a peach tree.
He thinks: "So we are fated to meet! Otherwise,
why would this hairpin have fallen into my hands?"

He stays awake that night to admire the pin
with its lovely scent of sandalwood.
At dawn, as the mists are clearing
he sees Kiều searching on the far side of the wall.
He dresses quickly, and creeps towards the spot
where she must be, and says aloud:
"Oh, look, I have found a hairpin.
How will I ever find its owner?"

Kiều calls across the wall to him:
"But I have found something better yet.
That hairpin is worth a little money, true –
but more valuable by far is the honest heart
of one whose instinct is to return a trinket
that a stranger must have lost."

Kim says: "But we walk beside the same wall
and under the same trees. We are not strangers,
we are neighbours. I am grateful to your perfume,
because its drifting has led me to you.
Since last we met, I've dreamed of this moment:
that was a long day.
Wait here. I want to tell you some secrets."

He rushes home to fetch a few things:
a pair of gold bracelets, a silk scarf, and a step-ladder.
He climbs the wall as if stepping into the sky.

There can be no doubt. It is the same girl.
He stares at her.
Uncomfortable, she looks away.

He says: "We met once, by a lucky chance:
since then, my heart has yearned for you.
Look – I have grown thin as an apricot tree.
Day after day I lived with fading dreams
until no longer believed
that I would ever see a day as happy as this.
I spent a month with my head in the clouds
and a second month knowing I'd rather die
than give up hope of meeting you.
But now that I've found you, I'll ask my question:
can your bright mirror shine on this broken fern?"

Kiều thinks for a moment. Then she says:
"My family is poor as ice and pure as snow.
When it comes to love, I will do as my parents wish.
Your hot words burn like fire,
but I am my parents' child. I cannot answer you."

Kim says, "Today it is windy, tomorrow it might rain:
in springtime, who knows what will happen next?
Your reasonable words will hurt me,
but how can my hurt help anyone?
Just give me a sign that you can love me
and I will speak to the matchmaker.
If not, then the potter's wheel has thrown me off,
and that's the end of my short and pointless life."

Kiều listens to the soft lullaby of his words:
something pleasant there, but something fearful too.
She says, "Everything you are telling me is new.
But since I am the source of all your trouble,
I will accept everything you say and I will match it.
I will write your words in gold.
I will carve them in stone."

And this unties the tricky knot that binds his heart.
He gives her the silk scarf, and the gold bracelets.
He says, "One hundred years from now, everything we've said
will still be remembered. Let these little gifts
witness the eternal promise of our love."

There is a sunflower fan in her hand.
She gives it to him.
In return, he gives her the gold pin
that had fallen from her hair.
This exchange of gifts unites them forever
as surely as if they have been pressed together
and fixed with lacquer and glue.

But there are voices in the house behind her,
so they flutter like leaves in the wind.
Kim scurries down the ladder. He is away to his books;
Kiều goes back to her bedroom.

Nguyễn Du (1765-1820) was a Vietnamese diplomat who reluctantly accepted an official position in a regime that strictly prohibited the printing and dissemination both of 'national tales' and of poems 'associated with profligacy'. While ambassador to China, he clandestinely adapted into Vietnamese an historical novel about a courtesan and prostitute whose life seemed to resonate with his own. *Đoạn Trường Tân Thanh* (*New lament, broken heart*) was first published anonymously in 1815, on woodblocks, in traditional Nôm script – the earliest version in modern Quốc Ngữ script dates from 1866. It rapidly grew in popularity and (often known simply as the story of Kiều) has become an enduring inspiration for a nation that has repeatedly been forced to endure oppression and foreign occupation.

Janet Sutherland
Assemblage des Beautés

Bone monkey has set up shop in the airing cupboard.
It's warm in there. Silverfish take refuge in his skull
and slide around his ribs. Worn sheets have ruched between
his bones like the petals of old roses – *Assemblage des Beautés*
for instance – so cherry red and full it almost seems
there is blood again and a heart beating like crazy.

Sean Elliott
Domestic Behaviour

Apparently cats may share
two owners unaware
that both are feeding one
domestic animal;
it's comforting to learn
that cats, like us, are far
from scrupulous and turn
for lovers anywhere.

Daljit Nagra
Kalaka Gora's Penal Braggadocio

How oft do mates bang on at length about
   how well they're hung, they grab their crotch then slash
   the air, then chuck an arm firmly around
   a chum while necking Stella till they're lashed.
To tell the truth, I'm really not well hung
   and thus I hide from mates my prince's state,
   this conk is king of my poor frame, no trunks
   would lunchbox find to bank a lady's gaze.
And yet I hope the guys won't feel too down
   should I recount I praise my lover's power
   of head to rise above the *corrrrr!* from louts
   who check her out too long like sonnet writers.
In the sack, she bares her soul and adds: *Ooo love,*
you're the first to make me whole with your subtle touch!

Alan Brownjohn
Ludbrooke: His Cash Flow

Varies between a pose of fastidious care
And a pretence of letting it all hang out.
Which to face the world with is a real dilemma,
But he mostly inclines to the first of the two options
As the second might tempt him to leave a wrong impression
Of letting go in every situation
– Which could be dangerous; not to say expensive.
But he does have days of abandon – false abandon –
So that friends might say, "Whatever you think of Ludbrooke,
He has his own kind of 'dash', his own 'panache'.
To be 'devil-may-care' at his age is a talent
Vouchsafed to few, you have to envy him."
Yes, his friends might say that; though he has yet to hear them.

Margo Berdeshevsky
Wind

The woman goes to parties, parties are important to her, events
                 in situ for worthy conversations, cells
of life, in her body, in her left breast, something is growing, her
                 new lover has noticed it, she's postponed
a probe, a day, a week, a month. *Life*, she says often. *Life*. A favorite
                 catchall word for her delicate antennae's thrill
to irony, to grace, to passion, to misery, subjects all too rich for
                 dinner's sauce, still her plate is full,
and she eats, like a hungry sparrow, sips *champagne*, her other
       favorite word, sees breeze through every glass, and toasts to *life*.

How like a Grecian warrior boy with battle scars nipple to navel –
                 standing in a window of any season, any
bravery – that other woman with no breasts, now, but slice marks
                 healing on her field of stitched skin
cut, now, her second one severed – she stares down fate. They're
                 poets – eye to eye. Cut the marble to free its
interred wings – the sculptor Michelangelo knew, still not knowing
                 what winds can do to beautiful women.

I saw an angel in the stone and carved to set it free.

From the notes of Michelangelo.

Dan Burt
Momentum

Surgery, chemo, hairy combs,
Time congealed in waiting rooms
Where strangers wonder if they'll live
Clutching lover or relative,
Rogue cells rallying again
To salt sections of a brain:
Prostheses, wigs and summer balls
Feign indifference to it all.
When medicine has nothing left
Life still negotiates with death.

Boats are pulled, sheets cover chairs,
The Season dwindles into air
And body gives disease its head:
With skin slackened as it spreads,
Liquid nourishment tube fed,
Vocal cords and bowels dead
Morphine soothes what few will shed
Until, the fly-wheel whirled to rest
All ripen into food for pests.

Man imitates cosmology
From heaving groins to elegy;
Primeval bang to nothingness
From emptiness to emptiness
We cling relentlessly to breath.
In the camps few chose death.

Susan Wicks
The English Couples

Is it the quality of light
leaking from the walls of buildings
like an unkept secret, or the weeping planes
trailing their thin gold
in the water, swans drifting together and apart
between the leaves that float
like lace on the still surface? The bells
cough out their quarter-hours
over gilded scrollwork; fur
fringes the mouths of bridges.
A sudden smell of drains
gusts on a comer, as if a door
had swung suddenly open downstairs.

High over northern Europe, I saw the town
slide like a coin under my dark wing
and remembered stars
shaking in water: now I'm the one that blinks
and slips sideways as a street blurs
to a scallop of stepped gables
where the gentle English couples
walk up and down.

Simon Armitage
The Last Panda

Unprecedented economic growth in my native country
has brought mochaccino and broadband
to where there was nothing but misery and disease,
yet with loss of habitat the inevitable consequence:
even the glade I was born in is now a thirty storey apartment block
with valet parking and nail salon.

They scrape DNA from the inside of my cheek
and freeze it, "just in case".

To the world I'm know by my stage name
and am Richard to family and friends, but never Dick.

Well-meaning tourists visiting the Cavern,
throw pastries and pieces of fruit
despite notices regarding my sensitive nature and strict diet.

I cried all night when John was shot,
rubbed the tired circles of my eyes till they turned black.

Please do not tap on the glass.

The sixties did it for everyone, I mean EVERYONE,
and what people failed to grasp about Chairman Mao
was that despite the drab-looking suits
and systematic violations of basic human rights
he liked a good tune as much as the next man.

Liverpool's a great shag but you wouldn't want to marry it.

They named a potato snack in my honour and also a small family car,
how many people can say that?

Fans write to me from as far away as Antarctica
and I insist on responding personally. In fact my "sixth digit" –
an enlarged wrist-bone which functions as a thumb –
means that handwriting comes easier to me
than it does to many other creatures, for example the Rolling Stones.

If I didn't believe there was one more hit record in me
I swear I'd end it now.

In the dream, there's still a Paul and a George
somewhere in the high valleys of Ganzu Province,
classic period white shirts and black ties,
mop tops down to their shoulders, strumming away.

These sun-glasses have prescription lenses and are not just for effect.

Reviewing my Wikipedia entry I note that "Yellow Submarine"
and "Octopus's Garden" anticipated the absurdist trend
in rock 'n' roll by at least a decade.

Every first Tuesday in the month the lady vet gives me a hand job
but due to the strength of the tranquilizer the pleasure is all hers.

Years ago they brought Yoko to the doors of my cage
but it wouldn't have worked; I let the slow
snowball of my head roll sadly eastwards
and stared towards the Himalayas.

In the whole cosmos there's only me.

What hurts most isn't the loneliness but the withering disrespect:
as if they'd dropped a couple of bamboo sticks into my paws
and I'd just played along.

Omar Sabbagh
Poppies

For Maha Sabbagh, with more understanding than...

Poppies. Plastic for the war-dead, paper for the war-dead,
Each year I'm disabused by the blankness of their red.
I blink, like a human being, unfixed by the gases,
Sulphur-yellow, the massive yellowing of frailty
And disease. A straight *dirtiness* for the masses
Of dead: legionnaire amongst a skidding legion
I bellow, lung-strong... (like a human being).
But then again, knee-deep in swells of blood.
Look at these swells: they've blood on their hands.

Fred Voss
Freud Surfs Amazon.com

Freud
is looking over at me from the screw machine he's been running
for a week since he got hired as a temp worker
to replace Garcia who's in jail for drunk driving
Freud doesn't have a beard yet
looks about like he did in that photo in the late 1890s right after
he discovered

the unconscious
"I got your book on Amazon.com and read it,"
Freud says
to me at lunch at my workbench where I munch a sandwich and
read Finnegans Wake

we lock eyes
I don't know why I'm here
why I've given my life
to machines that can cut off my fingers in a split-second
machines that pound and swing and chomp into steel
like butter
and men who never read anything but the spread sheets to football
games

they bet on
"You will never understand it," Freud says
guessing
my thoughts the way you'd think the father of psychology
might
"It's big
Sophocles got in touch with it
Dostoyevsky
Tennessee Williams
Bukowski
It's the unconscious"
Freud taps me on the shoulder

why
did I drop out of Ph.D. school to make a poor wage
at these greasy machines writing poems
for peanuts?
Freud winks at me
no one will believe his theory of the unconscious
until WWI
and he goes back to his screw machine to feed it another rod of
                                        steel
to think
the father of psychology learned to run a screw machine just so he
                              could work next to me

for a couple of weeks
maybe I'm not crazy
after all.

Pascale Petit
The Little Deer

After Frida Kahlo

Little deer, I've stuffed all the world's diseases inside you.
Your veins are thorns

and the good cells are lost in the deep dark woods
of your organs.

As for your spine, those cirrus-thin vertebrae
evaporate when the sun comes out.

Little deer too delicate for daylight,
your coat of hailstones is an icepack on my fever.

Are you thirsty?
Rest your muzzle against the wardrobe mirror

and drink my reflection –
the room pools and rivers about us

but no one comes
to stop my bed from sliding down your throat.

Kay Syrad
"Registering their flora / their fauna"

(*from Elizabeth Bishop,* Crusoe in England)

The fog-harvesting beetle has smooth, peaked surfaces
    with troughs of water-repelling wax –
it tilts its back and water-droplets roll into its mouth;

the larvae of the stag beetle live inside dead oak for five years;
    in the iridescent blue beetle the scales are stacked,
layer upon layer, light accumulating;

only in polarised moonlight can the dung beetle
    roll its ball in a straight line;
and the water-beetle carries fish eggs on its fins:

and so she makes you wait,
    her colours placed, geometry in the fold-up
chairs in lantern light – *two different lanterns, the lights*

swinging, and there – the *rose red rock roses*;
    listening, and waiting, not even waiting – until all
the winged Madeira beetles have been blown out to sea.

Ruth Fainlight
Facts About Ants

The fierce grip of black ants' mandibles
clipped together the gaping sides of a wound
in my ancestor's thigh. As the jaws clamped
shut, the writhing bodies were twisted off.

To cure her rheumatism, my great great
grandmother was eased into a tin bath
where a nest of ants had been boiled. Their
formic acid made the water dark as iodine.
(These days, more likely, she would order
Chinese Ant-venom Extract on-line.)

Tons of cement were poured down the vents
and chimneys of an ant city, to map the structure.
Then, with the same care it was built, the earth
around was dug and shifted, to uncover

galleries, garbage pits, pastures where workers
milk honey-dew aphids, air-conditioned
fungus gardens and larvae nurseries,
the queen-mother's chamber. No single mind
conceived this triumph of the collective.
I contemplate it with awe and fear.

A colony of forty thousand ants
has the same number of brain cells as a human.
Ant brains are the largest among insects.
Each has the processing power of a computer.

"Go to the ant, you sluggard, consider its ways
and be wise," were King Solomon's words
in the Book of Proverbs. But ants yawn.
In Japan, they say that an ant-hole will collapse
an embankment; in Africa, that not even
the sharpest ear can hear an ant's song.

John Whitworth
Wittgenstein's Show And Tell

All I can do is show a thing and say
This is what human life is like, or so
It seems to me, or so it seems to me
That that's the way of things, the way they go.
What do you think? Say yes if you agree,
Smile and say yes. All I can do is show
The way it seems, or so it seems to me.
The play's the thing. So watch the bloody play.

This is what life is like. This is my life.
My life, your life, our lives, they're all the same,
Like chalk and cheese, sweet jeez like day and night,
Like mad and not mad yet, like wrong and right.
Smile and say cheese, sly smiler with the knife.
My life is wrong but that is not the game.

Elizabeth Barrett
From Stone Psalms

I
Isle of Slingers, lands of the King, white tablet
        licked by salt, dipping and tilting gently
        south in wrinkles of light from the east.
        Carved by time from a single stone – no one
        between stone and the Crown Court of sea
        and sky. Ack-ack. Ack-ack. The gulls
        squabble, hold the high air's Leet.

II
Pulpit Rock. Hallelujah. Dead Man's Bay. Sea-struck
        land with one bound stone on a shingle bank.
        Waves heave themselves onto the beach
        and pull back. She can hardly stand – picks
        her way through pebble heaps dragging at her feet.
        Above the clatter disturbed stones whisper:
        here is the way to slowly end, to disappear.

V
Lines of weakness. Gullies running through the whole
        sequence. Vertical fractures where the land slid,
        toppled north-north east to south-south west,
        up-dip. She leaps them like a long ear, joints
        crossing at right angles beneath her oustretched
        feet. This is where pig places are cut, wedges
        driven in; the surfaces turned higgledy-piggledy.

VI

Wedding. Jump three times over the iron rod; that one
　　　used for drilling. Wear a hat. Stand up straight.
　　　Sing *The French Song*. Sink plugs and feathers.
　　　Drive the wedges in. Ream up! Ream up!
　　　Pig place. Pig face. Her cheeks are grooves
　　　of cuneiform. The clouds have blown to stone.
　　　The whitecaps carve themselves upon the sea.

XII

In Suck Thumb Quarry the flowers are flying;
　　　powder blue petals in the air. Silver studded
　　　blues. Trefoil. Eyebright. There are winning
　　　chains around the bleached blockstone.
　　　It is sweetly stacked. Scooped walls sink
　　　to an apron of white, the bottom of the world
　　　sublime. On the north wind she hears bells ringing.

Some of the details in the Psalms are drawn from Peter Trim's *The Quarrying of Portland Stone* (1991) and Rachel Barton and Peter Revell's *Portland Stone Experience* (2005).

I   *Isle of Slingers* is the name given to Portland by Thomas Hardy who described it as 'carved by time out of a single stone'. The Royal Manor of Portland is directly answerable to the Crown; a Court Leet, comprised of representatives of the Crown and tenants, is still in existence.

V   Rabbits are believed to be omens of bad luck, blamed for rock falls in quarries. Local superstition suggests that calling rabbits by their proper name brings bad luck. Pig places are grooves which were cut into the base of the block of stone; pieces of pig iron were inserted into these grooves and four wedges were then placed between each of the 'Pigs'. The wedges were hammered by quarrymen until the block was prised away from the main layer of stone.

VI   At local weddings the groom would traditionally jump three times over an iron rod, or 'jumper', used for drilling. Those present at the ceremony not standing correctly or wearing a hat would be fined and the monies given to the groom. Traditionally, 'The French Song' was sung by quarrymen to ensure unison while wedges were being struck. Plugs and Feathers are a more modern device used in splitting blocks; these are placed in a series of pre-drilled holes. 'Reaming up' describes the moment when the block is prised away from the main layer of stone.

Peter Carpenter
Orion

You have to see me to believe me or so I'm told.
I was up there when Dorothy was writing her journal:
Moonlight lay upon the hills like snow. Examine me now
and remember how your father fixed my position
in his calculations over Essen before the incendiary drop.
He thought I'd gone, but I came back for him years later,
unceremonious, no big deal, after that poached egg
on toast he'd fancied and a Sunday repeat of 'Morse'.
On his side of the bed I touched him – sent him tumbling
past the face of the alarm clock, luminous, circa half
four in the morning. Had he been able to part the curtains
he'd have spotted me back up there, a nonchalant thief
on a clear night lining up for the identity parade, ready
to hold his gaze as sirens and blue flashing lights broke the peace.

CENTREFOLD

I'm looking at "the future".
– *Patrick Dubost*

Under The Influence

MENNA ELFYN

T. Gwynn Jones was born in Gwyndy Uchaf, Abergele, North Wales in 1871, the son of a hill-farmer who loved literature and who taught him to compose poetry at an early age. He died in 1949, having brought Welsh verse from the Celtic twilight into a golden age. He stood alone in the vanguard of the literary renaissance at the beginning of the twentieth century, giving Welsh poetry a presence and the language a future.

In Wales, poetry allows you a key to a kingdom. Yes, you can actually become a king – of verse, that is! A Crown is given at the National Eisteddfod for a free verse poem and a Chair to a poet writing an ode in strict metre. These coveted ceremonies are seen by some as the pinnacle of the Bardic year. To become a chief poet is therefore both a national and a poetic honour. As for T. Gwynn: when he won his first National Eisteddfod chair in 1902, and his name was announced, under a pseudonym of course, to a hushed audience, there was more than a little *frisson*. Although he had heard that he had won the Chair, he'd taken a train that morning to attend a friend's wedding.

That winning ode, 'Ymadawiad Arthur' ('The Leaving of Arthur'), was deemed a stunning departure, as the poet had reworked the well-known story of Arthur's journey to the Isle of Avalon, which he called "Afallon ei hun sy felly". This means "As the isle of Avalon itself is so", a kenning that is itself in *cynghanedd* (strict metre). Although heavily influenced by Tennyson's 'Morte D'Arthur', the ode prophesised a national awakening and revival, with the wounded king being taken to the otherworld of Afallon. The poem seems to have appeared at just the right time. Wales was tiring of religious themes and this gave a certain edge to Welsh verse:

> Draw dros y don mae bro dirion-nad ery
> Cwyn yn ei thir [...]
>
> Over the waves there's a gracious country
> Nor in that land lingers lamentation;
> Whoever comes there, no old age or pestilence
> Strikes down, for the clean breeze of freedom
> Keeps every heart of us nimble and merry,
> As the Isle of Avalon itself is so.   (translated by Tony Conran)

A romantic when he set out as a poet, T. Gwynn Jones was a restless spirit who wanted to shake up the establishment. In 1910 he wrote in the periodical *The Nationalist*, "I think I shall not be far wrong if I say that the bardic tradition has stood in the way of the greater development of Welsh Poetry." But how did he influence me? I never took to these myths and never sought to write epic poems, let alone to be part of a Bardic circle: something which seemed anathema to me as a woman poet and later as a feminist. In the seventies, my writing was more akin to the tone of American poets such as Robert Frost, Emily Dickinson, Elizabeth Bishop or the struggles of Anne Sexton. I started out writing in the late sixties, the era of wanting to embrace the world by fighting oppression. Abhorrence of the Vietnam War, the necessity of the anti-apartheid movement, and the urgency of language campaigns were all a backdrop to my writing and the tone of my voice also differed from that of T. Gwynn, as in this poem translated by the late R.S. Thomas:

'Speak up' is, of course,
the command to speak English.
I sentence myself to a lifetime
of sentences that make no sense.
No pronunciation, no annunciation –
inflection. I am infected
with dumbness. I can neither lampoon
sing in tune; much less can I
intone [...]   (from 'Song of a Voiceless Person to British Telecom')

But in my head, and in my heart, were the riches of his odes. One magnificent poem tells the tale of a twelfth century Welsh prince wanting to escape the feuding of his brothers, crossing the Atlantic and perhaps discovering the Mandan Indians. This gave rise to my desire to imagine a worldwide brotherhood and sisterhood just as 'Madog' had done, and to escape the bigotry and small-mindedness of belonging to a small nation. And in this, I identified with T. Gwynn's romantic notion of other worlds. The poet himself *is* Madog, his ship *is* his imagination – and 'Madog' embodies his reaction to the war in Europe. T. Gwynn once said he was a pacifist with the emphasis on the 'fist': so much so, that he in fact walked out of chapel one Sunday morning when the preacher started to pray for the success of the British in the First World War.

Here are the concluding lines of 'Madog', a poem which ends in despair. The ideals of a better world perish along with the prince:

Rhonciodd y llong, a rhyw wancus egni'n ei sugno a'i lyncu,
Trystiodd y tonnau trosti, bwlch ni ddangosai lle bu

The ship swayed with a fierce energy then, swallowed alive,
The waves gashed over her, a gap showed not where she'd been.

'Argoed', written in 1927, is in my mind his most memorable work; a story based on the Roman conquest of pre-Christian Gaul, in which an entire tribe chooses suicide rather than the humiliation of Roman rule. Here, the poet once again translates that idea so that it will resonate with Welsh experience:

Argoed, Argoed of the secret places,
Your hills, your sunken glades, where were they,
Your winding glooms and quiet towns?

Ah quiet then, till doom was dealt you,
But after it, nothing save a black desert
Of ashes was seen of wide-wooded Argoed.

Argoed, wide-wooded... Though you have vanished
Yet from the unremembering depths, for a moment,
Are you there, unconquerable soul, when we listen –

Listen in silence to the wordless speech
Where the wave of yearning clings to your name,
Argoed, Argoed of the secret places?   (translated by Tony Conran)

This kind of poem about doomed civilisations inspired my generation, in the sixties, to ensure that the Welsh language had a future. I can't say that T. Gwynn was directly responsible for my imprisonment on a number of occasions for non-violent language campaigns, but the thought of a language and culture disappearing completely did spur so many of us on to fight for a bilingual Wales, something which is now almost within reach.

A recent poem of mine, from *Perfect Blemish*, though a much happier poem than 'Argoed', is I feel close to the gleam captured in his work. Written about seeing the sea when we'd visit it as children, it must have been influenced somewhat by T. Gwynn's fascination also with oceans:

Y cynta'i weld y môr

Bod y cynta' i weld y môr
Dyna'r agosa y down [...]

Seeing the Sea

To be first to see the sea
Is the closest we may come
To open-eyed discovery.

There she lies, a temple
Helping us draw the line
Between heaven and earth,
Nothing and oceans.

We travel gladly towards her laughter
Reaching the skirt-hem of her stories,
Where her tongues tell truths.

For a time, we stare, not understanding
Her depths, this divinity who will
Not reveal herself, hugging her secret

And see anew that a sea
Is no less beautiful because ships
Founder on rocks, because, look
In her split-second waves

We grow younger with each frisson;
Seeing the sea
For the first time
Is the closest we may come
To the wonder of eyes opened.

T. Gwynn Jones's last volume, *Y Dwymyn* (The Fever), published in 1944, testifies to the fact that he became a Modernist in later life, as he wrote even more starkly of his fear and despair of humanity. In many ways, the romantic and patriarchal poet is overturned here, where he rails against the futility of war and its treatment of women. Two poems stand out in my mind as being so unsettling that they have not yet been fully appreciated by Welsh readers. The first is 'Pro Patria', which draws attention to the horrors of war. In hospital, the narrator tells a Welsh nurse his experience of witnessing, in the midst of war, the rape of a woman:

'Hurry up! You're damn slow at it laggards!'
Said one of the twenty, quite hoarse;
From the house came Jobkins and Jaggards
With their faces all red and coarse;
Juggins and Muggins and Snoddy,
Damning 'these bloody Boers';
'Taffy!' called one, as I got up,
'Buck up! There's some fun indoors!'

'Twenty seven of those devils had been there –
And she, who till then had been pure-
Damn it all! My soul was on fire
Though not better myself, to be sure,
The sound of their lecherous sniggering
As the other two walked through the door
And the lust and the greed on their faces –
I don't recall any more.

'Stand back!' I remember I said that,
'Or I'll brain you, by God, that I'll do!'
As I raised the butt of my gun up
I remember the oath I swore;
I don't know where I aimed each bullet
In that frenzied quarter-hour
But the noise grew quiet. I looked down
And saw two wads of brain on the floor!   (translated by Elin ap Hywel)

The last piece I want to mention could have just as easily have been written after 9/11, or the recent attack on Mumbai, but in fact appeared in 1934/1935, and is called 'Dynoliaeth' ('Humanity'). It describes the destruction of a city; the aftermath is told in dramatic detail. There is, as always in T. Gwynn's poems, brute force but also a priest, hermit or scholar on the sidelines. In this poem, as in so many others, he realizes his belief that the poet deals with what is eternal in man and is concerned with mercy as a redeeming force:

It was night in one of the old cities,
Heiress of every daredevil deed of the long centuries,
She who had gilded herself
With the loot of the lands she despoiled,
In the days of her power
She who knew then she was no longer
The greatest city in the world.
It was night in the old city.

Fog enveloped her,
Her streets lay empty,
Dark and silent
Not a crack of light
Not a peep of pomp or poverty,
The network of sewers where ran
The pity and filth of life's twists and turns
From the veins of her wealth and its glance of glory
[...]   (translated by Gillian Clarke)

As an antidote, I wrote about the need for every country to learn the language of its neighbour. I published this after returning from Bled in Slovenia, where I led a workshop for refugees who had to flee Bosnia in the early nineties:

Bloedd
(Let the World's People Shout)

Have you noticed how time-free a person is
When approaching a new language?
Yes, you stumble over consonants,
Postpone vowels,
Encumbered with all the armour of your longing
For the conquest of expression,
And yes, your tongue is like
A baby bumping along on its bottom.
Well then, let each of the world's people learn
The excommunicated language of its neighbour,
Yes, creep and crouch in corners,
Lose sleep in messing it up,
Since this is how tenses will be deleted.

The past will not come fluently on tongue,
The language of today with stay. It will sue for peace,
Pull down all the barbed-wire verbs.
The imperfect will never be so perfect
As when it ceases to exist.

There will be no time for spreading hatred,
Since the tribes will be overcome
By the riches of all the founding stones –

And through the babies in Babel
A yoke will be raised, a United Languages heal
In freeing oneself, freeing in sowing the seed.

If the world beyond Wales knows little today about T. Gwynn Jones, he made absolutely sure that Wales should know the world. He was both prolific and polymathic, and single-handedly translated Goethe's *Faust*, several of Ibsen's plays, Greek and Latin poetry and Irish literature into Welsh. He wrote essays, libretti, novels, plays and literary criticism. He was a true European, at a time when it wasn't terribly attractive to be so. (In 1928, he said that "we'll all be English when we stop writing in Welsh".) His wide-ranging work and agnostic world-view made him a towering figure, unrivalled in Welsh poetry. Although for many years a journalist and then a librarian, despite his lack of university education a personal Chair – Professor of Welsh at the University of Wales, Aberystwyth – was created for him. Not bad for a man who had left school at fourteen! In fact, there were plans afoot to nominate him for the Nobel Prize for Literature. But as soon as he heard of this he put a stop to it, asserting that his work wasn't good enough. This modesty, his deep sensitivity and accompanying bouts of melancholy are all evident in his work. The early writing sought a "lost paradise" and his later work was a quest for serenity.

Two words I overuse because of T. Gwynn Jones are *nwyd* – passion – and *noeth*, meaning "to be bare, or naked". He laid his passion bare and also gave me the riches of his inspiration, the commitment to still search for that "lost paradise". He was also, to me, a poet of the light – and what can a poet ever hope to achieve but to bear witness to, to catch, that light?

Commissioned by Julian May for BBC Radio Three and broadcast on 4th December 2008.

References & Further Reading

Tony Conran, *Penguin Book of Welsh Verse*, Penguin, 1967
Tony Conran, *Welsh Verse*, Poetry Wales Press, 1986
Menna Elfyn, *Eucalyptus*, Gomer, 1995
Menna Elfyn, *Peffaith Nam, Perfect Blemish*, Bloodaxe, 2007
M Elfyn & J Rowlands, *Bloodaxe Modern Welsh Poetry*, Bloodaxe, 2003
Gwilym ap Gwynn, *T. Gwynn Jones, Cyfres y Meistri*, Christopher Davies, 1982
David Jenkins, *Thomas Gwynn Jones*, Gwasg Gee, 1973
T. Gwynn Jones, *Caniadau*, Hughes, 1934
T. Gwynn Jones, *Y Dwymyn,* Gwasg Aberystwyth, 1944, (University of Wales Press, 1972)
Iwan Llwyd & Dafydd ap Myrddin, *Gêm rhwng dau fileniwm*, Carreg Gwalch, 2004

BALKAN HAIKU

Dejan Bogojevic (Serbia)
from Unpublished Poems

While we utter
verse after verse,
night falls.

*

Church bells –
Their melody makes me closer
to my forefathers.

*

Wilted flowers.
The fire crackling
more and more quietly.

*

A mountain road:
music that appears
first silent then loud.

Translated by Danielle Bogojevica

Primož Repar (Slovenia)
from Woods, Icons

A vessel full of flowers –
at the very bottom,
a quiet expectation.

*

Two faces on the fiery
saddle of the sun,
riding into a new day.

*

I watch you. Your eyes
part the darkness
of the last possibilities.

Translated by Polona Kolenc

Luko Paljetak (Croatia)
from Hairdresser For Chrysanthemums

Another day another
day another day another
day another: thank you!

*

At the end of a letter
there's always room
for a few more words.

*

At the end of the verse
the petals from drenched roses
drop off.

from Haiku In War

I still check the time
on the ruined
bell tower.

*

An ant is trying
to haul away
a dislodged church bell.

*

Look, even the frog
has put on its
camouflage uniform.

*

From amongst the spring onions
a gun barrel
suddenly rises.

Translated by Deljka Letica

Aleksandar Prokopiev (Macedonia) *from* Sparrows On A Wire

He's picking figs –
a love offer
from tree to mouth.

*

A shot in the night.
In the divided city
we all are victims.

*

Long ago letters,
bitter-sweet crumbs
from an abundant table.

*

Sunday in autumn...
The phone ringing, persistent
as the rain.

Translated by Dimitra Dafalia and Irina Ivanovska

Modern Poetry: A Way Of Happening Or Of Non-happening?

STEVEN MATTHEWS

When my Dad's mother died, my Nana, my Granddad reverted to an earlier version of himself. Moved by the local authority out of the council house he and Nana had shared for sixty years, and put into a small bungalow, he became again the army-engineer who had been a Desert Rat with Montgomery in North Africa, then in Italy, France, and Holland. He had his hair cut short. He got up earlier each morning, polished his shoes and shaved with his cut-throat razor, then sat himself down at his flimsy formica-topped kitchen table for his egg and toast.

But, before he switched on the radio and began eating, as on one visit he shyly told me, he first took a moment, a moment in which he read out a poem aloud, keeping my Nana before his mind's and heart's eye:

> If I should die tomorrow
> It will not mean Goodbye
> For I have left my heart with you
> So there is no need to cry.
> This love that's deep within me
> Will reach you from afar.
> You will feel it all around you
> And it will heal the scars.
> I love you all my family
> So always do your best,
> But don't turn away and forget me.
> For life's span is just a test.

He had chosen the poem from the collection in Nana's handbag after she died. For what I hadn't known is how that tight-clasped bag, one of several which had pinched my fingers when I'd been told to get my pocket money from it as a child, had also held something which my Nana thought most dear. Amongst the seemingly endless supply of mint imperials and tissues to wipe ice-creamed hands, Nana kept small notepapers on which she'd copied out poems from the local newspapers, the *Essex County Standard* or *Colchester Evening Gazette*. They were often commemorative verse penned by local people or, presumably, derived from anthologies, and sent in to the paper on birthdays or wedding anniversaries – or they were poems like this one, seeking to offer consolation to those left behind. To a woman like Nana, who had left school at the age of twelve and been sent into domestic service, they clearly offered some sense of the possibility of saying or understanding something which she could not herself have put into words in this intense and concise way. That they were always, unbeknownst to most of us in the family, carried carefully folded away in her handbag makes me think that she saw these poems as constant companions, constantly there as possible ways of interpreting whatever, in a normal day, might befall her. Hers was a long tough life in a very tough part of Colchester; the poems offered what sense of understanding it there was.

What moves me for the purposes of this piece is the fact that, after she'd died, my granddad took on *this* aspect of her life as the way of staying in touch with her. I want to hold in *our* mind's eye those early-morning rites, the moment of quiet before the everyday begins, the need to speak with the lost beloved, and the use of poetry to do so. For it is startling that this poem offered a man as inarticulate as my Granddad the way and means of doing this. Granddad could sit at his table and speak aloud this poem every morning, for the three years until he himself died. Such moments, the taking of time to speak with Nana, are what I wish to talk about: partly as an act of commemoration of that background from which, without my knowing it, my love for poetry probably comes, but more expansively as a general discussion about the significance of poetry, and of those moments we might make for poetry, amidst the noise and distraction of the cynical and rushing modern world. Why are poems so important at moments of personal grief, or of national tragedy – the Soham child murders, Hillsborough, rail disasters? I want to suggest that it is because they are set to a different kind of time, that they create time where we can think differently, time where we can commune in different ways. Time, the time poetry takes, and the time poetry makes happen amidst the accelerated happenings around us, forms the key thread I want to follow through the debates and examples here. Time as what binds us, as what poetry especially alerts us to; the time of poetry as a necessary way of talking to, and about, what could not otherwise be said.

Poets and critics from a variety of national and political perspectives have made much, in the past hundred years and more, of the significance of poetry like that in the newspaper copied out so carefully by Nana. In an essay on 'Myths, Metres, Rhymes', Ted Hughes sees such writing as a way of declaring "solidarity with 'the common people' [...] in the native British tradition. It emerges from pure melody as no other form does, tending, in the most intense and admired specimens, to archetypal themes opening backwards into religious myth." For Hughes the major Romantic writers, including Wordsworth, Coleridge, and Scott, brought back into English poetry, in other words, a sound pattern and thematic core that had been silenced by the more refined and courtly poetry which had taken over in England since Renaissance times. It is a rhythm and metre which has spread in more demotic and popular versions like the Nana-poem. Hughes's own poetry harnesses something of that original revolutionary impetus.

From another context entirely, but to similar ends, the Australian poet Les Murray has written about the origins of *his* nation's poetry in the nineteenth century:

> From the end of the first quarter of the nineteenth century until the end of the first quarter of our own, there was an enormous mass of verse published in newspapers and likely to be read by high and low alike. [...] Many of the earlier ballads had their first appearance not in the mystical mouth of the Folk, but in some metropolitan or country town newspaper.

In this passage, Murray is characteristically sharp in resisting a national mythology which is founded upon the so-called drover poets like Banjo Paterson wandering the outback and rhyming definitively about the new land which is Australia, that "mystical mouth of the Folk" dismissed in the last sentence. But he celebrates, here and elsewhere, the function of this newspaper verse in achieving a *different* sense of folk tradition which might lead, he hopes, eventually, to an Australian republic:

> This republic, the one we have to discern, is inherent in our vernacular tradition [...] part imaginary and part historical, which is the real matrix of any distinctiveness we possess as a nation, and which stands over against all of our establishments and colonial elites.

In the post-colonial situation, then, a sense of the role of poetry as an everyday presence which works to define a nation's consciousness is, as it is for Hughes when thinking about the "native British tradition", an enduring force. This kind of poetry still appears in Australian newspapers. The sense of vernacular tradition given by Murray, as one being mediated through the tight forms of locally printed verse, goes along with a celebration, in both Murray and Hughes, as well as in many other twentieth century poets, of the role that the imagination plays in conceiving the new national possibilities: "part imaginary and part historical", as Murray puts it when defining his ideal version of an Australian republic.

Poetry as anti-establishment and anti-elitist: but also as enlisting the best possibilities in people, as providing a space or middle-ground in which *all* areas of society might meet to discover a shared emotional and national consciousness. The political desire to discover such energies in even the most established and canonical poetry was strong throughout the twentieth-century and continues today. The Anglo-Irish poet W.B. Yeats, for instance, claimed to hear, within the refined pentameter lines of the opening of John Milton's Protestant epic *Paradise Lost*, the echoes of a 'folk poetry' consonant, presumably, with the vernacular tradition – which he sought to present as a version of a potential Irish republic at the turn of the twentieth century. Contemporary Irish poets, from Seamus Heaney to Ciaran Carson, Eavan Boland, and Paul Muldoon, have subsequently shown a continuing openness to the folk tradition as exemplifying a national continuity and distinctiveness. And which in its turn generates some of their own poetic approaches.

I have included the deliberate outlandishness of Yeats's claim in this list of valorisations of 'the common people' in order to sound a note of warning. For, of course, in each of the instances I have noted, from Hughes, Murray, Yeats and contemporary Irish poets, there are other agendas operative – or, rather, some might say, a confusion between different agendas. In each case, including the Hughes, a political drive, a nationalist impulse, has become entangled with aesthetic recognition. This aesthetic recognition is partly about the sheer liveliness and memorability of the shorter lines of this kind of newspaper or folk poetry, when compared to the more expansive and sophisticated metres which hold sway in mainstream English writing. But the political agenda in each case is clear. To the extent that all three of these writers – Yeats, Murray, and Hughes – would claim that poetry makes something happen, or at least that it is an instrumental part of moving a political and national debate forward, they are making that claim from a partial and professional point of view: one only partly keyed in to the concerns of the 'folk' or the 'common people' they seek to use as an example.

The title of this piece, about poetry as a way of happening or of non-happening comes, of course, from a pivotal moment within twentieth-century poetics. Pondering the achievement of Yeats in his elegy, the English poet W.H. Auden famously wrote that the Anglo-Irish poet's impact, whatever his political ambition, had been minimal:

Now Ireland has her madness and her weather still,
For poetry makes nothing happen: it survives
In the valley of its saying where executives
Would never want to tamper; it flows south
From ranches of isolation and the busy griefs,
Raw towns that we believe and die in; it survives,
A way of happening, a mouth.

As many commentators have noted, this is a fabulously complex passage of writing about something which initially seems straightforward: poetry, it seems to say, is unlike other forms of language, such as that used by business executives, ineffective and obscure. It is like a river flowing through a deep and dark gorge. In commemorating Yeats, Auden might be seen, then, to take a very modern view of the traditional honorific nature of the elegy, and to dismiss Yeats's political ambitions, as he does at the start of this part of the poem, as "silly".

But, if that is what Auden is trying to say through his poem, he has found an enigmatic and inexpressive way of doing so. Why does this river flow south, we might ask? What does he mean by "ranches of isolation and the busy griefs"? Why "ranches", in a poem about Ireland and an Anglo-Irish poet? What is the precise distinction being made between the phrases that poetry makes "nothing happen", and that it is "a way of happening, a mouth"? How, we might ask, does the one occur without the other? The whole picture is famously further complicated by the fact that this second section of Auden's elegy for Yeats did not appear in the first printing of the poem in an American journal, but only from the time of its reprinting in a London newspaper in April 1939. As Auden's biographer Humphrey Carpenter has remarked, what occurred in the meantime was that Auden spoke at a dinner to raise funds for refugees from the Spanish Civil War, and that his speech was extremely successful. But Auden felt overwhelming disgust at the notion of becoming a public orator in this way, and went and added this second section of the poem as a way of awkwardly distancing himself, the poet, from the public world of charity and politics. Poetry is an event in itself, on this reading, but is not one likely to affect other, non-poetic kinds of event, in which the poet feels uncomfortable making pronouncements. Auden might, under this aegis, be seen to be taking proper action, removing the confusion between poetry and politics, or poetry and public events, which I described just now in relation to Murray, Hughes and Yeats. His might be seen as a *proper* sense that poetry is remote from the more immediate actions of the "executives" and business people of the world. But this is to ignore what he *means* by poetry as a "way of happening".

Once again, we might note the professional interest which Auden has in seeing poetry as "a way of happening, a mouth", one which seems to create further contradictions as this elegy proceeds. By the end of 'In Memory of W.B. Yeats', in fact, the poet has regained his confidence in the power of poetry to affect those around, as he directly addresses Yeats:

> Follow, poet, follow right
> To the bottom of the night,
> With your unconstraining voice
> Still persuade us to rejoice;
> [...]
> In the desert of the heart
> Let the healing fountain start,
> In the prison of his days
> Teach the free man how to praise.

These final lines are carved on Auden's own gravestone. What they offer is an assurance, in Yeats's own ballad-like metres, of the fact that, even if it cannot found a new national possibility, poetry can bring relief to the arid emotional and constrained intellectual situation of the modern individual. Whatever the debilities of the modern condition, the erosions and entrappings of time and its prisons – and whatever the limited role which Auden feels poetry to play amidst other noise – these lines still attribute to poetry a continuing power to provide emotional and religious uplift, to make us "rejoice [...] to praise". Or, rather, Auden enjoins the spirit of Yeats to convince us of these things. He yearns for it to be so.

If I am left uneasy about the uplift of such commemoration, it is because of the fact that, once again, and whatever the political impetus of these final lines, the poem finds its sense of possibility from speaking to itself about itself – that, whilst it is not ignorant of the constraints under which we all live in the modern world ("the prison of his days"), it still values supremely the "unconstraining" (note the active adjective) power of poetry. There is, once again, a professional immodesty involved, in other words, one which *presumes* the importance of poetry as a given, if only we can – as Auden claims – value poets like Yeats properly.

I think it safer, amidst such confusions about where the value and purpose of, and ultimately the *audience for*, poetry reside, to look at things from the other way on. Andrew Motion's recent reflective piece in the *Guardian* on his decade as Laureate makes an interesting readjustment of the terms of these kinds of debate which, it seems to me, is to be admired. Motion claims that his motivation as Laureate had been derived from a sense, since proven correct, that "The audience for poetry is much larger than it's usually held to be[...] and that a far larger number of people [beyond those already engaged] could [also] take poetry into their lives." The basic notion that poetry speaks to many, and that it could speak to more, often in spite of the national curriculum or the expectations of the university and other academies, and often despite what poets themselves might say, is fundamentally true. In order that it can speak to more people, it seems to me that it is the responsibility of schools and universities to address and stimulate the taking of poetry into lives in whatever way is most immediate to them.

But in order for this to be so, it is important to recognise that poetry, to return to the moment of Grandad's reading at the breakfast table, also demands time and space, and *makes* its own time and space. Time in poems, as in music, is notoriously different from time as it is lived in the everyday world. Rhythmic variations in poems alter the normal pace of things, our sense of time passing. Our lives are bounded by time, and it is the difference in timing between poetry and everyday speech that dramatically brings us up against these limits. In this lies its vital way of speaking, and of commanding our attention. This is something which the best modern poetry, pressured by the fiercely accelerated time in which contemporary lives are lived, the speeding up of our hours and days, is particularly alert to. The time of modern poetry is largely a resistance to the breathless way in which we are meant to respond to the constant stimuli around us, from the computer game to the harassments caused by the rapid fire exchange of email, flashing billboards and bullet trains.

I want now to spend a while focusing on work by the American poet, Jorie Graham, because, as I hope to demonstrate, there are specific technical aspects of her kind of writing which forcefully dramatise this issue of the timeliness of poetry, the time it takes and makes for us creatively. To me, one of the best collections of new poetry of the past decade has been her book *Overlord*, which appeared in 2005. The title word, 'Overlord', becomes in Graham's hands a clever pun, since it refers us both to history and to religion. Operation Overlord was the name given to the Allied invasion of Europe on the French beaches in World War Two. But "overlord" of course carries the full burden of religious potential. To this end, Graham returns us to six dates when, as the titles of the individual poems inform us, in the early morning she makes attempts at "praying".

In the first of these attempts, that dated June 8th 2003, the poem's speaker draws upon the confusion of those Allied landings, in which many men were killed as their boats were washed up on the wrong beaches. Graham establishes this confusion as a marker of the ways in which humanity is unable to keep a direct line between what it desires, such as the conquest of Nazi-dom, or the drive towards religious understanding or faith, and the means to achieve that desire. As she recounts herself attempting to pray, Graham's speaker in the poem envisages the whole countryside around where she lives in northern France as being populated by the ghosts of the men killed during the invasion:

> [...] the spirit does or does not die
> with the body, that being maybe the only real question left us,
> besides 'us', the other great mystery, whether any one of us
> can even touch an other one of us, even here, naked, trying to get back
>   to sleep, chairs and tables
> pushing out void, taking up room, *I tell it*
> *as I see it* says the young man holding the gun, while I
> keep counting my numbers out – when will I have enough
> to make it through, to fall asleep – as now again I
>   have to start over
> where a shot from out there shatters
> my count... [...] Then suddenly,
> terrible, losing my place – ghastly, spilling, whole night sky
> unravelling – and *where* was I reaching, panicky, trying to catch the
>   outermost number, the one I
> just had – where was I – where is it – oh lord it is a
>   small thing, no?, to have to
>   begin the count
> again...

Here, as throughout the book, Graham associates the attention involved in prayer, and the time it takes, with the need to take control in and over circumstances which threaten to invade her and the poem's concentration. History is out there, somewhere, beyond the bedroom, and effectively beyond the poem. But history continually breaks into both spaces, as in the "shot" heard in this passage. The narrator finds it hard to sustain the space necessary to the act of praying, as even the furniture in the room fills areas she needs. The ghostly "young man" who suddenly looms into this void with a gun is almost a principle of direct utterance and action ("*I tell it / as I see it*"). And this throws into further relief the complex meanderings and looping progressions of the poem's dramatised speaker, moving continuously on from subject to subject without sentence-breaks as her mind meanders and turns back on itself. In contrast to that young man, this speaker increasingly panics as the passage progresses. She is presumably an insomniac, desperately counting to fall asleep, but sleep eludes her. She feels the whole world falling apart around her and, as a result, she is becoming more and more "lost". She seeks, as she puts it, to keep "counting my numbers out", which might be taken as a pun upon the other activity she is engaged in, of course, throughout these moments: which is the act of writing of the poem itself, counting *its* numbers.

This, like all of Graham's work, is a poem in which the action of the words, their "way of happening" if you like, is continuous with what they are set to describe. But, rather than the settled interaction traditionally central to the act of praying, the address of human words to some god, this is writing which cannot escape from its own modern lostness. Where a "lord" does appear, in the final lines, it is seemingly almost as part of an exasperated, almost blasphemous, outburst or challenge – "oh lord it is a / small thing, no?, to have to / begin the count / again". The extremely awkward line breaks here dramatise the inability of the poem's central voice to establish a true and straightforward relation with a higher possibility. As a part of this sense of disengagement, doubts emerge, again awkwardly expressed, as to whether it is possible to establish intimate human contact, "whether any one of us / can even touch an other one of us". That phrase, "an other one" brings a curious impersonality, a lack of personal identification, to the relation between lovers in this situation.

Graham seems to me to be a vital poet of our times because she recognises that, of these apparently-modern questions, scepticisms, or debilities, amongst which in this volume she also includes AIDS, global warming and GM crops – amongst all of this corruption of traditional orders, balances, and relationships in the world – poetry *must* continue to make its attempts at prayer, even at the level of self-communion. Hers is a poetics in which the movements of the speaking voice dictate and determine the flow of her lyric/dramatic rhythms or "numbers". Her reading of history, not least the history of the invasions which give her volume its title, is that accepted acts of male heroism are predicated upon a hinterland of mistaken directions, of actions leading nowhere: and that these archetypal Second World War scenes have been repeated, at other levels, in the subsequent sixty years.

This does not prevent poetry from having much to say about the impact of this indirection. It also does not prevent it from saying much about the need to *take time* for this to occur; time to be enacted and demonstrated in the strategies which the poems adapt. And this *different* sense of time is also a politics, manifest in the poet's taking responsibility not (as in Murray's or Hughes's or Auden's examples), *for* what might happen in the world beyond the poem, but *to* what has happened and is happening: a vital difference. It is a responsible kind of poetry, a responsible form of poetic happening – which we must make time for, as the performances in *Overlord* suggest.

Graham's poetry is the latest example of a modern American poetry of resistance, founded upon a sense of the presences and absences with which the acts of writing and speaking with poetry might engage. It brings to the fore particularly the moral impact of evoking those from the past or present who seem to speak and act through the work. Graham's poems, in other words, partake of the elegiac mood and tone of the twentieth- and now the twenty-first centuries, in which the mighty violences of history shatter the coherence and direction of earlier literature. To that extent, such writers understand a complexity about the performance of poetry and its relation to history which demands our special attention, but which repays the care and time we might spend, learning to hear it. Modern American poetry, partly because it is unafraid of difficulty therefore, earns its moments of revelation in ways that the more circumspect yet assertive modern British voice, as exemplified here by Auden in Part 2 of his elegy to Yeats, often does not.

Such complex insights seem remote from where I began in this discussion, the early morning scene at the table in which poetry seems to have been, for Granddad, the only possible form of speech with Nana. And yet I would argue that in Graham, more perhaps than in much contemporary British writing, there is, as in newspaper verse, little condescension towards the everyday, humdrum nature of things, the normal activities of the commonality of people. There is in these contemporary American examples a refusal of language which might, through its own overly poetic character, set poetry apart from a people – an 'us' – or a normal speaking voice: however syntax gets contorted to convey the time of the poems' small miracles. Nor does Graham give up on the possibility that 'gratitude', praise, or faith, might not be discovered in, or emerge out of, such normal daily activities. They sustain respect towards their subject-matter, and towards that language which is necessary to render revelation a real possibility. Such writers take a long way round via their technique, as we have seen, in order to establish that truth. But the medium becomes their particular means towards obtaining it. The poems quietly make space and time in the everyday, in order to effect their transformations.

Such issues, it seems to me, lie at the heart of the recently published and absorbing-to-read correspondence between the American poets Elizabeth

Bishop and Robert Lowell. The question is of the relation of poetic technique to lived experience. Throughout these letters, full account is taken of the alien-ness of poetry as a form of human activity, but poetry is also recognised as one form of human behaviour in which truth might be revealed. Indeed, in what was to be the last letter he wrote to Bishop, Lowell returns explicitly to this issue, whilst recognising that the *truth* to be discovered in poetry lies at the *heart* of the multiple variety of possibility which reading poetry might offer:

> We had a dreadfully pedestrian PEN Club meeting here – 'The truth of the imagination'. All middle-aged people who have published two books but can't write, can't talk, but want to talk or at least hear people who can't talk talk. The intoxicating thing about rhyme and meter is that they have nothing at all to do with truth, just as ballet steps are of no use on a hike. They are puzzles, hurdles, obstacles, expertise – they cry out for invention, and of course in the end for truth, whatever that is. It's queer, though, Lawrence's Figs is de gustibus as true and surprising as Herbert's Affliction. But the task of composition is different. No more.

Of course, what drives Lowell's free-wheeling wit here is what impels everyone's correspondence to some degree: implicit lament at the absence of conversation in person with Bishop, to whom his letter is addressed. It is a lament heard again and again across the decades between Lowell and Bishop, a constant litany of urgings by each to visit the other, to make the time in busy lives and love relationships to do so. Here Lowell, in Bishop's absence, makes up talk to talk to her. He does so, initially, by talking about the uselessness of much literary talk. He dazzles, with his line about ballet shoes on a hike for example. What is impressive though is that, as in many other places in the letters from both poets, the impatience displayed in the opening scene at the PEN Club rapidly gives way to a recognition that, instead of discussing such wafty subjects as "the truth of the imagination", it is necessary for poets *rather* to talk about the mysteries of technique. *They* must take a properly professional approach to that matter which, in other hands, is mere wasted verbiage.

Technique gets in the way of expressions of truth, Lowell says. But technique is necessary to exposing the truth. It is "different" from many things, including the act of reading, which in itself offers instructive wonders. D.H. Lawrence's poem about eating figs can offer almost as religious an experience of taste ("de gustibus") as the Renaissance parson George Herbert's meditations upon *his* conscience, and upon the difficulties of faith in his several poems called 'Affliction'. What both of these tastes depend upon for the reader is "puzzles", "hurdles", "expertise": the expertise of the *poet* in overcoming the obstacles of technique in order to present truth responsibly.

In this instance from his final letter, Lowell, who was in many ways irresponsible towards his technique and disrespectful towards the human subjects in his poems, rises above himself. He does this many times in the correspondence with Bishop, as though her constant distance from him, and the consequent spontaneity of his writing as the only way of talking across the gap, frees him into his better self. For witty transformation of mundane and silly talk, such as that at the PEN meeting, into serious attention to poetic technique is not something Lowell always attained in his poems. This seems to have been something Bishop, herself so careful over these matters, and so revelatory, was regretfully aware of. Her elegy for Lowell, called 'North Haven', picks up these things movingly:

> Years ago, you told me it was here
> (in 1932?) you first 'discovered girls'
> and learned to sail, and learned to kiss.
> You had 'such fun', you said, that classic summer.
> ('Fun' – it always seemed to leave you at a loss...)
>
> You left North Haven, anchored in its rock,
> afloat in mystic blue... And now – you've left
> for good. You can't derange, or re-arrange,
> your poems again. (But the Sparrows can their song.)
> The words won't change again. Sad friend, you cannot change.

This is again writing about talking, talking with the now-forever-absent friend. Bishop's verses capture Lowell's hurtling, bragging talk. They capture the uncertain temporalities of gossip and reminiscence (was the classic summer in 1932? Or not?). But Bishop's elegiac poem also becomes the best means of reflecting on 'talk', picking up as it does on Lowell's commonly-used word "fun" as something he was, in his frequent periods of hypermaniacal mental distress, unable to cope with.

Awfully and sadly, at the end of the first full stanza quoted here, that sense of being left at a loss sparks the grieving of the elegy's last verse. Lowell left the paradisal place and time where all of this fun which is being recounted happened, North Haven. Now, terrible in the proper sense of the word, a line-break dramatises this event as it follows the hiatus of the hyphen "now – you've left / for good". This emphasises the punning resonance of that little phrase, "for good". It means eternity, but it also means relief that Lowell has in effect gone to a place in which he is better off than in the turmoils of his life. The poem sees this and bestows it on him. On the other hand, this is hardly a matter for satisfaction on the speaker's part. Nature can more-or-less continually repeat or recreate itself. The individuality and particularity of humans, their irreplaceability in time, means cruelly that this natural abundance and evolution, the ability to change, escapes them. Lowell, the inveterate tinkerer with his own poems, constantly revising them on the page and in his poetry readings, so destroying their technical revelations, is as it were caught out in death, where he "cannot change". The poem's final rhyme is a chilling judgement on the lost "sad" friend, as the ability to "de-range" is snubbed by the chiming phrase "cannot change".

I have made much here of the proximity of modern poetry to the absence of the loved one, to the presence of death, which it seems to want both to embody (the "void" which Graham frequently writes about), and also to shut out. It seems, as here in Bishop's elegy, that poetry has become again what historically it often was – a *particularly* appropriate way of speaking to, and reflecting upon, the dead. History, the past, and those who have suffered in it, and been killed, have become increasingly the things which poetry has been drawn to. The losses of the past century work as metaphors for the broader disappointments, inconsistencies, or lacks of meaning under which we all suffer in this modern age. To a certain extent, as mentioned earlier, it is because twentieth-century and contemporary poetry, following on from but also intensifying and re-scoring Victorian work, seems particularly to be a poetry of mourning: for lost potential, for lost voices, for those presences, like the dead soldiers in Graham's *Overlord*, who haunt the history of the past hundred years. To a certain extent, also, it is recognition of the lost consonance between words and things. It is the sense of a lost time in which such consonance might be discovered and celebrated. And yet poetry, when it finds a telling form and rhythm, when it makes its once-and-for-all time, does continue as a special way of carrying this burden and possibility.

As I hope to have dramatised in this discussion, it seems to me that the most worthwhile modern poetry, and the *distinctive worth* of it, comes in its sudden, startling and often unlikely ways of leaping across those gaps of separation and loneliness which form the particular characteristic of modern life. It consciously recreates and stages a present connection to what would otherwise be lost or at least absent. These poems incorporate into themselves a recognition that, especially now, where words have become so debased as a currency, it is difficult to leap across those gaps. It requires work. For the poet, this is the labour of technique; for the reader, work at listening to the difficult, often intractable, issues involved. This intractability is not least found in the fact that the separations and bewilderments we often live under are best responded to by bafflement and silence. We are *all* rendered inarticulate before them. But if we take, and make, 'time'; and attend to the time taken by poems, whether they are Nana's newspaper verse or intricate literary writing, they become, for everyone, including those who could not otherwise talk about such things, consoling ways of speaking across the silence.

This is a short version of a talk given as a Public Lecture at Oxford Brookes University on 22nd April.

Patrick Dubost
The Words "The Future"

I'm looking at "the future". I'm sitting in the present and looking at "the future". I'm trying to see what's beyond, but "the future" is an opaque object. I get up and go round it. Gently. Does it take time to get round "the future"? ...And now I see "the future" from the back: I see "erutuf eht". "Erutuf eht" is only slightly opaque. I try, beyond "erutuf eht", to distinguish the present. I make out my empty chair. I tell myself, positioned in front of "erutuf eht" and further off my empty chair, that if I go back I'll see "the future", I'll see the future without inverted commas. I go back very gently and I see: "the future". Behind "the future" is "the future". Don't give in too quickly. I go gently round "the future" #2, I turn back gently and see "erutuf eht". I turn back gently and see "the future" #3. I stop for a while. I ask myself about the present. About the problem of the empty chair. After sprinting eight metres, I hurdle "the future" #3, then "the future" #4, and I continue running and jumping but I'm no longer worrying about the present or the empty chair. Until "the future" #10. And there: nothing more. Except, on the bare ground fifteen metres away: "finishing line". I jump "finishing line", so lightly. Lots of noise from the stands. (My ancestors, my descendants.) They make a hellish din. I'm still in the present. I turn back under the shouts and missiles. I see the perspective of "erutuf eht"s and right at the end, undisturbed: my chair is empty.

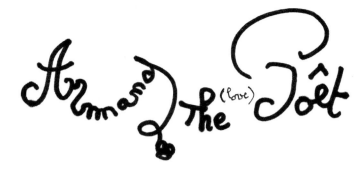

Armand The (love) Poêt

I COUNT
THE PRETTY
WOMEN
728
SINCE THIS MORNING

SHE CRIES
DO THE TORTOISE FOR ME
DO THE TORTOISE FOR ME
AND I DO
WHAT I CAN

THE GOOD LORD
SAYS TO ME
EVERY DAY LOOK AT MY
SUPER COLLECTION
OF PRETTY GIRLS

ALL WOMEN
MARRIED
TO SOMEONE OTHER
THAN ME
ARE
MISTAKEN

in love
I am
an autodidacte

the poêt
who knows how to talk
     to women
is an administrative
         poêt

advice
to a young poêt:
« write first,
        then love »

it's forbidden
to put all one's eyes
in the same basket

love poêms
written on the train
     (subset
of the general set
     of love poêms)

if you are
the one I love
lay
a bouquet
of flowers at the foot
of this poêm

to make
or not to make
love ?
a question
Shakespeare
asked himself
but didn't write

(he wrote another one)

(making love with you
is like being in a pedalo
in lake in paradise without being dead
and as many times in your life
as you like)

Armand Le Poête

SOUTH DEVON CELEBRATES POETRY

Acumen, the South-West's leading poetry journal, appears three times a year and is a celebration of poetry in print.

120 pages of poetry, articles and interviews from local, national and international poets. New features for next few issues are 'Seminal Poems', memoirs, prose debates and, of course, many new, readable poems. In past issues, the magazine has published international poets alongside others just starting out. A great mix of themes, styles and enjoyment.

Reviews of poetry from both large and independent publishers. Still only £12.50 for three issues.

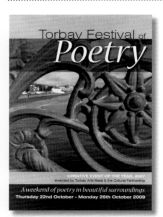

The Torbay Festival of Poetry, the only poetry festival in the South-West: a celebration of poetry too good to miss.

Over the long week-end 22 – 26th October 2009, up to 30 poets will celebrate the joy of poetry, past and present, through readings, workshops, open-mics, debates and other events. Join us for a weekend of poetic excitement and fun.

Event prices: many free, others from £3.50. Weekend ticket to all events (including a workshop, Festival Supper and lunch): £76.

Torbay Open Poetry Competition.

JUDGES: Mario Petrucci (ADULT SECTION)
            Alison Varndell (14 – 18 YEARS).

PRIZES: £700, £300, £150 (ADULTS)
            £200, £100, £75 (14 – 18 YEARS).

ENTRY FEE: £4 per poem (3 for £10) adult
            £2 per poem (3 for £5) 14 – 18 years.

For further information on any of the above contact Patricia Oxley on 01803 851098 or email PWOxley@aol.com or write to 6 The Mount, Higher Furzeham, Brixham, South Devon TQ5 8QY

REVIEWS

Fill out the form. Do it in bloody triplicate. Enrol.
– Arundhathi Subramaniam

House Of Flames

SAM LEITH

Tomas Venclova, *The Junction: Selected Poems*, ed. Ellen Hinsey,
trans. Ellen Hinsey, Constantine Rusanov & Diana Senechal,
Bloodaxe, £9.95, ISBN 9781852248109;
Mark Doty, *Theories and Apparitions*, Cape, £9, ISBN 9780224085281

"Only a true nobody can manage / to shoulder the weight of non-existence," remarks Tomas Venclova with sour brilliance in the opening lines of 'Henkus Hapenčkus, In Memoriam'. A note on the text inform us that this Henkus is just the nobody he describes – the non-name, attached to absurd birth- and death-dates, that stood as an advertisement in the window of a funeral parlour in Kaunas, in the author's native Lithuania, for decades. These poems tell us in grave and immaculate phrases about the erasure of the individual, the enormity – and enormousness – of history, the strong likelihood that we're going to die, and the curious hopefulness that comes from recognising the bone and sinew of your curse. Here are earnest, attentive and artful poems shaped by Europe's horrible twentieth century.

The strengths of Venclova's poems are also their weaknesses: their bone-deep solemnity; their insistence on dropping an anchor in history as a comfort in the face of, and a rebuke to, the vandals of totalitarianism. Donne, Herbert and Dante are here as literary lodestars; Theseus and Orpheus as mythological presences. "Someone had told us once that this site," he writes in 'The Eleventh Canto', "Like many sites, resembled Ithaca." That seems to me a very well poised, half-casual, semi-disavowed way of swallowing the epic.

Some poems have a feel about them of 'Union Dead'/'Near The Ocean' period Robert Lowell: a *paysage moralisé* described in a tough, defeated tone of voice; the poet's figure semi-effaced; the pressure of history, none too subtly, leaning in on the spaces of the poem. 'New England Harbour' – which echoed, for me, 'The Mouth Of The Hudson' – talks about "the uncertainty you have lived". In another poem, we see a man who "scoops up meaning in his hand, and washes his cancelled face". "You are indistinct, but the setting's explicit," a third poem warns.

This fine selection is divided into two – the first half, 'The Junction', comprising poems of the last decade, more or less; the second, 'Winter Dialogue', spanning the mid-Sixties to the mid-1990s. Translation duties on the former are divided between the editor, Ellen Hinsey, and the Russian-speaking Constantine Rusanov. The earlier poems are in versions by Diana Senechal. There's nothing unobvious to say about different translators – but it's worth reiterating, and this collection underlines it, that they give you different poets. There are three Venclovas here. Ellen Hinsey's Introduction describes a poet whose formalism produces poems that build stanza by stanza "like classical columns, which slowly rise towards the mythical silence where Venclova believes poetry begins and ends". Her own translations, though, seem more sinuous and idiomatic; Rusanov's more literal; and it is Diana Senechal's versions that give us the formal Venclova, rendering him ingeniously – though I've no way of knowing how faithfully – into villanelles, sestinas and what have you. Yet Senechal also gives us eccentricities – a rattlingly anapaestic poem without punctuation or upper-case letters; one set centre; one that uses a sort of incantatory anaphora. The monoglot reviewer can only read, admire what catches his fancy, wonder whether the true Venclova is so plural. Plural or not, what comes through all of these translations is that on song he's bloody good.

Can it be so many years, meanwhile, since Mark Doty's *My Alexandria* knocked all of our socks off? It's about fifteen, apparently. *Theories and Apparitions* is Doty's eighth collection, according to its jacket flap, and it has all the lyric precision and humour and poignancy you expect from him. These are poems to enjoy, easy but not shallow. You wouldn't maybe think that you'd discern Ginsberg and Wallace Stevens and Thom Gunn in so talky a poet, but you can in Doty.

The collection does what its title promises. There are a handful of "Apparition" poems (the poet spots Berryman eating lunch in a diner, Whitman in mid-town New York, and someone channeling Shelley in East Texas vowels), and a number of poems offering a "Theory" – of beauty, marriage, multiplicity, narrative, incompletion and the soul. All these "theories", so called, though, are rooted and indeed defined by the concrete details of life. The collection opens with a lovely piece, for instance, about catching sight of a bat ("fleeting contraption / speeding into a bank of leaves [...] little Victorian handbag / dashing between the dim bulks of trees"), and the difficulties of making a poem about it. Later, he applies the same jocose exactness to a peacock – "the epic / trombone-slide-from-Mars cry / no human throat can mime [...] the archaic poem of his tail".

These poems are offhand in voice, and marvellously full of the world. "Ligustrum, penicillium, / three ragweeds, fusarium, marshelder, pollen of timothy, sweet vernal, / cocklebur and feathers, dog and tuna, dust mite, milk and yolk" are what the allergist's assistant tests on the poet's skin, for example. Then there's the dementing Scheherezade of a Mexico City taxi driver, who so bores our hero and his boyfriend en route to the airport that

> [...] when we staggered out of the cab,
> hoisting luggage up onto the airport curb,
>
> I was too sick to even feel relieved,
> and Paul, gone a pale, peculiar shade
> like blanched celery – I do not exaggerate,
> although I have, for the sake of a good story –
> bent over and vomited onto the sidewalk.

Doty states, with a hip levity perhaps unavailable to Tomas Venclova though the sentiment is shared: "If beauty *is* burning, what could you save? / The house of beauty is a house of flames."

Sam Leith is a journalist and critic, currently writing a novel for Bloomsbury.

Forms Of Life

DOUGLAS HOUSTON

Derek Mahon, *Life on Earth*, The Gallery Press, £9.95, ISBN 9781852354619;
Nina Cassian, *Continuum*, Anvil, £8.95, ISBN 9780856464089;
George Szirtes, *New and Collected Poems*, Bloodaxe,
£15.00, ISBN 9781852248130

Derek Mahon's *Life on Earth* achieves the scope its title announces through the sea imagery that pervades it. 'Homage to Goa' clearly acknowledges the sea as *fons et origo* and sustainer of life on earth:

> waves smash on beaches for no obvious purpose
> except to deliver the down-to-earth palingenesis
> of multitudinous life particles [...]

While the book makes clear Mahon's virtuosity in complex, highly regulated stanzas, the imaginative primacy of the sea is perhaps clearest in the magisterial simplicity of 'The Clifden Road':

> West of Clifden on a cliff
> where sky changes into sea
> and sea to memory as if
> at the edge of a new world
>
> on the long hills of Clifden
> the green hills of Clifden
> I will lay down my grief.
>
> To accept death it must be
> that death changes into light
> that light changes into sea
> and sea into memory [...]

The consonantal and alliterative threads those lines interweave run seamlessly through to the close, typifying the rich musicality of *Life on Earth*.

'Biographia Literaria', an imaginative resumé of Coleridge's life, commands attention as surely as the mariner's glittering eye with the captivating music of its opening:

> A spoilt child shivers at the river's edge –
> night-hiding yes but anxious to be found,
> a troubled soul torn between fear and rage.

The collection's settings range widely through Europe, Asia, and America. 'Insomnia' is among its evocations of Irish coastal localities and provides a good example of the refreshingly innovative stanza forms that recur in the book:

> Scratch of a match
> fierce in the dark. The alarm clock,
> night-vigilant, reads twenty minutes to four;
> wide-awake, as so often at this dead hour,
> I gaze down at the lighted dock,
> trawler and crated catch,
> as if on watch.

The fourth stanza's "shrimps worship the stars" might have found a place in 'Homage to Gaia', the nine-part sequence central to *Life on Earth*'s ultimately celebratory concern with the interactions of nature and humanity. Throughout it, Mahon shares Auden's skill in using light verse to bear the most serious of meanings: the possibility of humanly precipitated ecological catastrophe:

> You will prevail of course
>   if in a different form;
> we go from bad to worse
>   just trying to keep warm.

The poem sustains that relaxed ballad form throughout its fifteen pages, bearing the reader easily through its engagements with technologies, natural phenomena, and metaphysical speculation. Its energetic variousness extends to a section that is at once a startlingly original tribute to the Icelandic singer Bjork and an apocalyptic take on Earth's melting ice caps:

> Up there where silence falls
>   and there is no more land
> your scared, scary voice calls
>   to the great waste beyond.

The imaginative audacity of Mahon's early verse and the meditative gravitas of more recent collections come together in *Life on Earth*. Its far-reaching technical and thematic vitality suggest his coming work will be well worth waiting for.

The poems in Nina Cassian's *Continuum* are selected from work written between 1947 and 2007. She has translated some from her many titles in her native Romanian. Cassian was exiled from Romania in 1985 after discovery of her satires aimed at the Ceaușescu regime. 'Remember', the first of the book's six sections, draws on earlier times, reaching back to the exhilarations of childhood through to intuitions of a ruthless state closing in as an idyllic holiday is shadowed by imminent threat:

> How did this day escape
> the aggressor's edicts?
> I'm not entitled to it,
>   my well being is not permitted [...]

> Let's savor it as long as we can:
> quickly, quickly, quickly.　　　　　　　('Summer X-Rays')

'Creatures from Inner Space' follows 'Remember', projecting psychologically acute states that recurrently derive their contexts and imagery from the conflict between political tyranny and the roots of personal identity:

> I had a lot of good friends,
> insane like myself.
> We attended gatherings,
> but society intrigued against us
> until we became enemies.

The book's third section, 'Travelling', contains similar elements of unsettling psychological exposure, but is better typified throughout its varied locations by the precise music and imagery of 'Nature', the opening poem:

> I closed another season behind me
> – the river was locking itself in armor,
> the woods were lacing themselves
> in thin silvery spider webs;
> winter was around the corner.

'Homages' is dominated by the hundred lines of 'Interpreting Bach'. This tremendous fugue of a poem conflates contemplations of the nature of music and biographical glimpses of Bach as paterfamilias, embedding the 'father' motif for its incorporation of Christian liturgy and God as 'total parent' to the heroically creative,

> who restore dignity and the coincidence between truth and beauty,
> the restless dialectic of the world,
> to those who give palpability to numbers and organize hope,
> to those who answer questions daily [...]

The collection's closing sections, 'Love's Boomerang' and 'Finale', find Cassian respectively taking stock of her long life in often astringent treatments of her loves and marriages and reflections on age underpinned by sharp intimations of mortality. The seven-part 'Letters' in the penultimate section is an enigmatic mosaic of everyday imagery and imaginings edging on the surreal. The poem drives home its repetitions of "I don't love you" as the last line of each of the parts, curtailing their imaginative flights with the emphatic bluntness of renunciation.

'Finale' maintains a counterpoint between reflections on the fragility of age and spirited celebrations of a life that triumphs in continuing:

> I, who never had any chances except the chance
> to live smiling, when, instead of hair or memories,
> insults and spit were running down my temples,
> – I, who was never in power, but had the power
> to exist and to embrace you, my enemy,
> and to be ready at any time to die,
> – I've always had the 'Haves' – having,
> had, have had, had had and Have. ('The Big Conjugation')

The range and power of *Continuum* will make clear Cassian's stature as a major contributor to modern and contemporary poetry to all who read the collection.

George Szirtes's work has always been striking for its wealth of visually realised details that function as stepping stones for the imaginative penetration of the worlds on to which his poems open. Considering the visual emphasis in his poetry in his valuable Preface to the book, he dismisses "the art poem" and finds a parallel for his work's essential qualities in the terms "punctum" and "blind field" from Roland Barthes's meditation on photography in *Camera Lucida*. The former denotes the focal detail of a photograph, the latter the whole world beyond the exposure's moment.

The punctum of Szirtes's poems and their fundamental humanity are often fixed in opening glimpses of solitary figures who offer ways into the surrounding fabric of lives, locations, and history: the major sequences 'The Photographer in Winter' and 'Metro' respectively begin their sustained recoveries of family history with "You touch your skin. Still young. The wind blows down the street [...]" and "My aunt was sitting in the dark, alone [...]".

Szirtes's mother, Magdalena Szirtes, is at the heart of these sequences. Her work as a photographer furnishes images for navigating the labyrinth of 1940s Budapest, while her deportation as a Jew to Ravensbrück opens directly on the *Nacht und Nebel* at the dark heart of twentieth-century European history. 'The Photographer in Winter' is dedicated to her memory, which haunts much of the book and can fuse with the elegiac shadow that periodically falls throughout it.

Szirtes balances his profound sense of life's fragility with poems of unbridled affirmation. 'In a Strong Light' celebrates "the everyday news / of bridges trees and grass", while 'Backwaters: Norfolk Fields' reiterates the moving simplicity of "How beautiful the place is" in gratitude for the landscape in which the poet lives. The Englishness to which he can lay claim is likewise held in balance by his identity as Hungarian. Being both, he can be fully neither, allowing an estranging detachment that contributes to his characteristic sharpness of focus.

Whether in strict forms – both traditional and innovative – or free verse, Szirtes retains an accessible clarity of voice. He can rise to an unflinching directness in confronting what some prefer to ignore, as in the treatments of the Tiananmen Square Massacre in 'Chinese White', Israeli territorialism in 'Second Decade: the People of the Book', and imminent financial crisis in 'Running man blues'. A number of the finest poems are pellucid lyrics that have the simplicity and impact of folk poetry:

> What arrives in frost and snow?
>
> *The broken branch, the late white night,*
> *a word or echo of delight.*
>
> What word is that?
> > I do not know.   ('Dialogue for Christmas')

"The metaphor of the journey through time forms a natural shape", writes Szirtes in his Preface. The book's journey through thirty years of published work compellingly explores the vast and innumerable private spaces that are the blind field beyond the public foreground of history and the present. It offers many rewards.

Douglas Houston is a writer and editor. His *New and Selected Poems* is due to appear next year.

Maters Of Life And Death

SARAH CROWN

Sharon Olds, *One Secret Thing*, Cape, £10, ISBN 9780224087841;
Ruth Stone, *What Love Comes To: New & Selected Poems*, £12,
Bloodaxe, ISBN 9781852248413

Sharon Olds is not a war poet. The woman who, with for example Anne Sexton and WD Snodgrass, has come to personify the confessional poetry movement has forged a career out of exploring a more personal battlefield: that of her "hellfire Calvinist" family. It comes as shock, therefore, to open her latest collection and step out among the soldiers and corpses of WW2. And while her taut snapshots of the conflict's human faces – the child watching a soldier smash her cello to pieces; the pilot who kept his flaming plane aloft while his crew jumped then "put the nose down / and saw the earth coming up toward him, / green as a great basin of water" – compel, they also confuse. Why has she brought us here?

It is not until we enter the body of the collection – where the action shifts onto more familiar, familial terrain – that a context emerges. The violent imagery of her opening poems works to set off ominous echoes in her depictions of a childhood in which her parents "labored as they had been / labored over, they beat us into swords". Furthermore, in a collection driven and shaped by the death of Olds's mother, the conflict-backdrop feels fitting: such is her mother's stature within her poetic universe that the destruction of multitudes is required to balance and realise it.

For, once again, mothers sit at the centre of Olds's poetry: her mother, whose love was an act of violence (who "tucked me in with a / jamming motion"), whose violence was ineluctably bound up with her love; herself as a mother, "free to think the thoughts of one in bondage" only when her daughter sleeps. This is, of course, well-trodden territory for Olds, but her own shifting circumstances suggest a new approach. In this collection, which interposes the birth and growth of her own children with her mother's slow sinking, her focus moves – subtly, essentially – from the emotional to the physical. The body itself – its frailties, its beauty, its ability to evoke tenderness and disgust – becomes her subject, in poems constructed of fittingly visceral, natural images. Birth is expressed as an unbodying (her daughter "had taken off my body – / that thick coat, cast / off"); death is a physical cataclysm ("like witnessing the earth being formed, / [...] seeing / the dry lands be separated/ from the oceans"). Her own mother, meanwhile, is acknowledged materially as "flesh that / gave me life", and such physical ties, Olds discovers, run deep: even when locked in battle, their "bodies called / to each other, brought each other bleeding".

The act that finally frees her from her mother's shadow is corporal, too. Olds softens her mother's "parched" lips, as she lies dying, with petroleum jelly; an action that, through its physicality, assumes a sacramental significance. "I worked", she says,

> for my motherhood, my humanhood I
> slid my forefinger slowly back and
> forth [...]

> [...] ran the salve in-
> side the folds, along the gums,
> common mercy [...]

This intimate act, rendered half-queasily in language that verges on the sexual, permits her, at last, a means of escape: by drawing as close as possible to her mother, "touch[ing] inside her", Olds gently, finally, breaks the spell of her influence.

Sharon Olds has written the introduction to Ruth Stone's *New & Selected Poems*, and the tribute is fitting: poetically, they share a common purpose. The texture of their poems, however, differs substantially: Stone provides a forthright counterpoint to Olds's dense emotional interrogations, setting out only, where Olds seeks to explicate. "Now the body rises to be fed" she says in a recent poem. "It knows its own. / It does not need my codes and maps. / It does not care what's hanging in my head." The end-stopped lines and relentless repetition speak of a poet at the end of a long career – a long life – who has moved beyond the need for equivocation or decoration. After the clutter and charge of Olds's attempts to unpick the relationship between body and mind, her bland clarity is as refreshing as a splash of cold water.

This clarity, though, is hard-won. The poems from her first collection, published in 1959 – just months before her husband committed suicide, leaving her to raise their three daughters – are quite different: formal, complex, lyric; supple with enjambment, ballasted by familial images (a sunset in which "sister slept like a rosy anchor / Fastening parents to a bench"; daughters "whose hearts are going / Higher, higher with your wild hair blowing"). In her next collection, *Topography*, love is overtaken by grief: the poems have been stripped of their bright ornaments, pared back to a handful of clean, pained images with which she endeavours to comprehend "the rubble of senseless longing for what was".

Because death halted the clock-hands for her, time is central to Stone. She pins her poems with dates and uses definite articles to draw particular times close ("that moment", "that day", "that winter"), seeking to make time work for her; to make the present real, or the past really part of it. The collection itself is arranged to confound time; by placing her new poems at the beginning so that they fall before her earliest work, she returns us, briefly, to a pre-lapsarian moment. But the illusion is short-lived, and the impact of her grief the greater for the warmth and brightness of the memories that fuel it. "We are balanced like dancers in memory," she says of her husband. "I feel your coat, I smell your clothes, / Your tobacco; you almost touch me." The brilliance of Ruth Stone's poetry resides in its attempts to surmount that tiny, deadly "almost" – and its simultaneous apprehension and acknowledgement of its insurmountability. This superb collection showcases a half-century's grappling with un-muted loss, rendered in startling, witty, unself-pitying lines.

Sarah Crown is the *Guardian*'s Online Literary Editor.

Delayed Debuts

JOHN BURNSIDE

Marie Etienne, *King of a Hundred Horsemen*, trans. Marilyn Hacker,
Farrar, Strauss and Giroux, $25, ISBN 9780374181185;
Arundhathi Subramaniam, *Where I Live, New and Selected Poems*,
Bloodaxe, £8.95, ISBN 9781852248246

That *King of a Hundred Horsemen* is Marie Etienne's first book in English comes as some surprise: Etienne is an important figure in contemporary French writing, both as novelist and poet; her book on theatre, *Anatolie*, won the Prix Mallarmé in 1998; she is a regular contributor to the leading fortnightly journal, *La Quinzaine littéraire*; most importantly, she is a true stylist, a writer of extraordinary clarity, whose skilful, multilayered narratives weave startling and lucid visions of the contemporary world – bus journeys, airports, the streets of Paris and Indochina – with the dreamtimes of history and myth. So the publication of this book, which won the National Poetry series' first Robert Fagles Translation

Prize in the US, is both long overdue and an extremely welcome literary event.

King of a Hundred Horsemen could be described as many things: a series of prose poems, a poem-novel or even, as the cover blurb puts it "a complex but playful reinterpretation of the sonnet form"; and it is, in some ways, all of these (even the latter: each of the book's hundred sections comprises fourteen prose 'lines', in which a subtle and very elegant system of chimes and echoes creates a logical and musical unity comparable with what we normally think of as a sonnet), but any such definitions should be treated as working guidelines to, rather than definitions *of*, what is, on every level, a wholly organic and unique work of art. Of course, comparisons will be made with other writers: like Marguerite Duras, Marie Etienne spent much of her childhood in Southeast Asia, and there are surface similarities between the two, in their treatment of cultural displacement and sexuality; one also thinks of Marguerite Yourcenar's concern with Asia and with myth and, though less obvious at a first glance, I sometimes find myself recalling Louise Bourgeois's short, quirky narratives and, perhaps, her wider world view. Nevertheless, Etienne is an original; a writer whose visions and observations, often in the form of a deceptively simple, yet searching question, haunt the reader long after the book is set aside – as in 'Section 8', a meditation on exile and the desire for return, in which the surprise of winter, after years in Africa, culminates in a whispered soliloquy:

> À présent me disais-je, tout sera différent, familier.
> La chanson très ancienne habite quelque part, dans le pays aimé.
> > > N'est-il pas vrai?

> (Now, I said to myself, everything will be different, familier.
> The very old song lives somewhere, in the beloved country. Isn't that
> > > true?)

We must hope that this translation is the first of many, and that Etienne's work will reach the Anglo-Saxon readership it deserves.

Where I Live, New & Selected Poems also marks the British debut of a poet who has been working in the field for some time, bringing together poems from Arundhathi Subramaniam's two earlier collections (*On Cleaning Bookshelves* and *Where I Live*, produced in India by Allied Publishing) and a selection of new work that, for those of us who have followed this remarkable writer so far, (albeit from a distance) are exciting additions to her oeuvre. Subramaniam's work is by turns laconic and passionate, often tender, always vital, drawing on family relationships (her poems about her mother, for example, are among the finest to a parent I have read), the clamour and sensual mayhem of city life, the journeys and homecomings of a sometimes solitary woman and, in the new works especially, the steady tension between the desire for intimacy (in all its forms) and the need to be alone. Throughout, her work is about choices made and not made, false choices offered and illusions sometimes painfully dismantled, sometimes carefully repaired; an early poem, entitled simply 'No' is answered, towards the end of the book, by the beautiful 'Learning to Say Yes':

> They matter,
> the minor questions –
> the smell of a new wardrobe,
> the eternal bus ticket
> in the bag's second compartment, the leer
> of the late shift security guard.
>
> Yes, Draupadi's sari is endless
>
> and there's no way to tame
> life's wild unstoppable
> bureaucracy
> but this:
>
> Fill out the form. Do it in bloody triplicate. Enrol.

That reference to Draupadi – when Dhushasana tries to undress her, after Yudishthira loses her in a game of chance, Draupadi's sari extends infinitely until her tormentor gives up from exhaustion – is indicative of the creative and sometimes playful way Indian mythology is used in Subramaniam's work, but also beautifully renews its metaphor's themes – questions related to Dharma, that is to say, to law and morality, and to the complexity of time – with marvellous ingenuity and wit. Indeed, Subramaniam is a poet whose appreciation of time is both vivid and poignant:

> Nothing like the cool
> morning sanity of leaf
> to remind you
> green is the colour
> of borrowed time   ('Reading the Leaves')

and she asks questions about morality and integrity that many poets simply refuse to take on. Yet she is also an extraordinary love poet, expanding our conception of what that means beyond the usual romantic notions, to include, not just other, but self:

> And then the nights
> when, turning over on the side,
> the arm reaches out
>
> and finds,
> with some ancient riverine instinct,
> a familiar lost tributary
> of self.   ('Return')

This is a remarkable book, from a remarkable poet; say 'yes' to it; buy it; enrol.

John Burnside's new collection, *The Hunt in the Forest*, is published by Jonathan Cape in August.

The English Line

ALAN BROWNJOHN

Andrew Motion, *The Cinder Path*, Faber, £12.99, ISBN 9780571244928

A ndrew Motion's last book, published in 2002, was *Public Property* – something he felt he might have become after accepting the post of Poet Laureate in 1999. The volume represented about five years' work – thus, two or three of them as laureate – but was still a selection. There were a number of poems which had "lived a sufficient life in the places which first published them"; a wise judgement on, for example, pieces like his *Guardian* memorial tribute to Ted Hughes.

Public Property was considerably longer than *The Cinder Path*, testifying to the effort Motion put into the activities he attached to the new ten-year laureateship. Awarding the T.S.Eliot Prize in January this year, Culture Secretary Andy Burnham praised Motion warmly for "fulfilling the Government's expectations", which should have caused candidates for the job to ponder the new relationship to government it might involve. Effort provided at the expense of his own poetry? If so, in terms of quantity only. The smaller new book is a weightier and better collection than the previous one and contains some of the best poems he has ever produced.

Motion lost out a little at the beginning by being an exact contemporary of Craig Raine and what became known (James Fenton's spot-on labelling) as the "Martian" school of poetry; his first book, *The Pleasure Steamers*, and Raine's debut volume, *The Onion, Memory*, were both published in 1978. The disarming novelty and verve of Raine's poems was applauded, the muted feelings and calm craftsmanship of Motion's attracted respect but little excitement: "a potentially very important lyric poet" was the best that one of his closest colleague could manage on the blurb of his next book. Only the poet Gavin Ewart, always discerning in his rare excursions into reviewing, had the courage to suggest at the time that Motion might turn out to be the tortoise to Craig Raine's hare.

Critical opinion might say that, with the spurts shown in *Dangerous Play* in 1984 and the *Selected Poems* of 1998, the tortoise had at least caught up. But if it has, it could be partly because critics have agreed with Motion's own conclusion and seen him as an honourable addition to "The English Line", the title of a piece here which endeavours to compress this entire tradition into just six lines of poetry. It's a list that begins with Wordsworth and Keats, misses anyone else before Hardy, Frost (yes) and Edward Thomas and stops at the earlier Auden and Philip Larkin. And being attached to this great parade doesn't necessarily do Motion a service because those are daunting talents to have so regularly cited as your antecedents. Which is why *The Cinder Path* is an encouraging development: an individual voice owing less to them than one might expect emerges in poems which almost immediately impress themselves on the memory.

It's not so much in the briefer, more gnomic examples, poems about bird names and bird behaviour, or cryptic childhood moments, or even the praised 'Harry Patch' sequence about "The Last Fighting Tommy", all of which contain some electricity but of a curiously static sort; 'A Dutch Interior' is intriguing, but far less charged than its wicked uncle, Larkin's 'The Card-Players'. The collection comes alive in five "found" poems which he fascinatingly converts into poems of his own, giving the source materials shape and dignity where others might just brandish them as triumphant discoveries.

One is a revealing passage from a letter of William Cowper about an air balloon which will not inflate, that melancholic poet in effect wishing he himself could be lifted up; another describes the failure of a team of "very powerful men" to fix a pier with the positioning of a new pile; a third narrates the nightmarish inability of a distinguished geologist to stop measuring and listing thousands of belemnites – "pieces too small to be of any use" – and publish some conclusions. Each poem is authoritative and absorbing in the handling of detail; each relates implicitly to the hazards encountered in pursuing the art of poetry.

Seven poems written in memory of his father end the book. 'Raven' and 'What Have We Here?' affectionately recreate episodes from his childhood, the others record the father's illness and death, anticipated earlier in 'Diagnosis'. 'Veteran' has soldier parent and poet son looking at a view (he is excellent at "views", real or symbolic) and recalling the past "waiting for the parade // of shadow-shapes to end". 'The Wish List' brings off, amazingly, the most difficult of tasks, a poem giving an inventory of small sentimental possessions his father might take "underground" – suit, season ticket, the "blotter scarred with hieroglyphs" – and ends with "your dying word / which, as you always meant, I never heard".

'The Mover' connects the father permanently with this obstinate machine, with which, after "pessimistic tugs on the starter cable", he manages to mow a lawn for garden cricket with his two sons. The boys wait while he stores the machine in the woodshed. "You always did come back, that was the thing. / As you also come back now in the week you died."

Motion has never been more sure and precise in treating subjects which simultaneously demand profound emotion and a proper reticence; or more touching and eloquent.

Alan Brownjohn's latest novel *Windows on the Moon* was published this spring by Black Spring Press. His *Collected Poems* were published by Enitharmon in 2006.

After Auden

STEVEN MATTHEWS

Glyn Maxwell, *Hide Now*, Picador Poetry, £8.99 ISBN 9780330456241

Glyn Maxwell's work carries forward Auden's concept of poems as forms of parable, as spaces in which the reader can engage, almost at a hypothetical level, with all manner of social and intellectual enquiry. It is bracingly unafraid of 'big themes', and unembarrassed about deploying traditional poetic devices, including personification. This is the case in the poem from which the title of his new collection is derived, 'Forty Forty', in which a child's game of hide and seek suddenly becomes overwhelmed by menace, when a struggle for control emerges between the male child counting, and a freaky interloper:

> [...] his confidence in a game he had
> quite misunderstood
> was awful to see and if History didn't correct him
> others would,
>
> so History ventured slowly towards him
> and – I don't know how –
> very gently took little hands in big hands and said
> hide now.

The tensions engaged here run across the book, as the everyday, either suburban or mythical, lives of its protagonists are suddenly confronted by forces or narratives which threaten or overwhelm them. This is a poetry of opposition, but also, as here, of shocking reversal, in which humanity seems unable to control the activities or ambitions it sets in motion. Often this is figured as a being-caught between many different 'stories', none of which seem to truly 'speak' to or for the individual, but all of which only leave the poems' speaker the more baffled and confused. 'One Thousand Nights and Counting' sees its protagonist positively victimized by its seductive story-teller; by the end of 'Tale of the Story-of-All-Stories', the poor done-over library-user has lost all ability to "understand / a word."

Maxwell gets a lot of energy, clearly, from inventing versions of what most alienates and harrows us. In the flickering sequence of poems voiced by Cassandra, for instance, this curiously and troublingly human character mixes charm and sexiness with outright nastiness:

> [...] you, by my lips, my ways, you think like me –
> wake with one face a sniff away forever,
>
> speak the lines she speaks at the moment she
> speaks these you speak and set your lips where she does,
>
> then you'll see nothing coming or becoming,
> and all will be so well.

In some of the poems gathered here, such as 'The Deal' or 'Element It Has', the level of abstraction can become irritating: we yearn for the direct, everyday voice of the victims of these threats straightforwardly to break through. Some of the most impressive work, in fact, comes in the more autobiographical pieces towards the end of the book, or in the fine elegy for Brodsky, 'A Walk by the Neva'. But there is throughout a sustained bravery in addressing the various lack of potential allowed by our modern situation, a bravery which is allied with a sophisticated and involving poetic intent.

Steven Matthews is a teacher and writer living in Oxford.

Poets And Artists

ANDY BROWN

Alice Oswald, *A Sleepwalk on the Severn*, Faber, £7, ISBN 9780571247561;
Weeds and Wild Flowers, with etchings by Jessica Greenman, Faber,
£14.99, ISBN 9780571237494;
Paul Muldoon, *Plan B*, with photographs by Norman McBeath,
Enitharmon, £15, ISBN 9781904634829

A Sleepwalk on the Severn is focussed on the moon – "mother of many rivers" – and how she changes the eponymous river and the lives of people living on it. The poem is structured in the repeating cycles of lunar phases. Scene setting, dialogue, elemental monologues and a Classical chorus constitute each movement. The whole ends with stand-alone poems from the poem's characters. Like *Dart*, *A Sleepwalk...* uses the voices of real people, blending personal stories with local stories, myths and elemental voices.

Oswald's style rests on the fulcrum of the present: speaking beautifully back to tradition, whilst forging a new vocabulary and syntax. Pulsing rhythms, rich and surprising imagery, unusual syntax and vocabulary, an engaging use of repetition: there is an unruly *made-ness* to Oswald's delightful poem. The poet herself is self-consciously present "*(that's me)... noting things down in my nightbook*", characterised as the 'Dream Secretary'.

There is humour here too. The Birdwatcher enters with "a wobbling light. A bicycle". When the moon speaks, she bemoans that headlamp: "Can't sleep. Little light left on". At the scene's end she rises slowly, "*shedding a weak, low battery light*". Later, the Birdwatcher looks at a bird through the wrong end of his telescope: "The little stint! Or is it?" He corrects his mistake, saying: "Not so little". Oswald's imagery is just right: a shriek cuts the air "shaped like a curlew"; a duck is "tucked in self-pillow", and an old man is "Dipped in old age up to the eyes". Instead of boat lights we see: "lights that speak ship language", alongside the dreamily surreal: "*Notice a feather bed being rowed across the river full of children*". Oswald's poem is all about that *noticing*: "Notice everything noticing". It shows how Oswald is a great witness, and why she is so worthy of "notice" herself.

Weeds and Wildflowers is a stunning, illustrated hardback. Jessica Greenman's etchings are detailed interpretations of plants, perfectly complementing Oswald's poems, which animate the plants as characters.

The poems are full of pathos: tragic and comedic by turns, they hold a mirror up to ourselves. "Stinking Goose-foot has grown human", it begins; "It could happen to anyone." And poor old Pale Persicaria lives "In a ditch by the roadside, / Full of sorrow sleepless", like a resolute Beckett character. Many poems play out troubled domestic narratives. Hairy Bittercress "ought to drink less // in her TV loneliness". Bargeman's Cabbage is, pejoratively, Bargeman's wife: "Her heart is damp / And tightly closed". Interrupted Brome is punningly sporadic in speech – "every time he speaks he pauses" – after a domestic trauma sweeping snow off his steps.

The poems are botanically accurate as well as metaphorically lively. Thrift sits on sea cliff: "Strained in the wind / In a pink old-fashioned hat". Imagery throughout is strong. Daisies are "choristers"; Violet's name "could only be spoken as a scent"; Helleborene is "a closed umbrella"; whilst Thrift contemplates "the sea's boredom. / Its bouts of atheism". Strong rhythms and rhymes are also prevalent: the life cycle of Primrose echoes the traditional, tribulatory form of 'Solomon Grundy'. This delightful book ends on a positive note, with Dense Silky Bent, who "just springs up green again and stares at the sun". Whilst there's sadness and pathos in this book, what you'll remember is its abundant wit.

Plan B is not a collection of poems about photos, rather a dynamic synergy between the two forms. 'To revert to Plan B', means that things haven't worked out the way we intended. It implies re-evaluation; taking stock, and places the present on a decisive knife-edge. The title poem explores this idea of life's 'best-laid plans'. Muldoon interrogates himself like a prisoner in "KGB headquarters", prodding himself "into a pool of icy water" – the icy waters of autobiographical poetry? The historical and political allusions twist and turn through Muldoon's poems, like the twists in the hank of rope McBeath has so beautifully photographed.

McBeath's photos echo the 'Plan B' subject-matter: doorways to secret gardens, ruins, statuary and graves each open a meditation upon time and being, as do the images from the natural world: starheads of sphagnum moss, ferns and forest floor flora, an apple tree, and windfalls. There is a temporal physicality to these images.

The poems bear Muldoon's signature, with complex formal arrangements and sequences, extraordinary rhymes, unusual vocabulary and punning, tense rhythms, and a seamlessly slick surface. Iconic figures from popular culture, history and myth, pop up in unlikely places. In 'A Hummingbird', Nora, "post-divorce", is throwing a party. Clearly a 'Plan B' scenario. Rhyme is prominent: "fidget", "digit", "widgets" and, yes, "midgets" all make an appearance here. As the women at the party gossip – "I'm guessing she's had a neck-lift and lipo", (another 'Plan B' strategy) – their chat is both high- and low-brow. Vibrators are mentioned in almost the same breath as *Finnegans Wake*: "You know I still can't help but think of the Wake / as the apogee, you know, of the typo" – a very funny scenario and line. This is Muldoon doing something new; perhaps that's the point of having a Plan B.

Andy Brown is Director of Creative Writing at Exeter University. His latest collections include *Fall of the Rebel Angels: poems 1996-2006* (Salt) and *The Storm Berm* (tall-lighthouse).

Rut And Root

VIDYAN RAVINTHIRAN

Roddy Lumsden, *Third Wish Wasted*, Bloodaxe, £7.95, ISBN 9781852248284; David Constantine, *Nine Fathom Deep*, Bloodaxe, £8.95, ISBN 9781852248215; Claire Crowther, *The Clockwork Gift*, Shearsman, £8.95, ISBN 9781848610323; Sarah Wardle, *A Knowable World*, Bloodaxe, £7.95, ISBN 978-1852248192

"You bastards!" Roddy Lumsden begins his fifth collection with a poem which takes the kind of invective spouted by middle-aged grumps and makes it fizz with imaginative energy – a forthright address to 'The Young':

> reaching the lighthouse in record time,
> pockets brim with scimitar things. Now
> is not a pinpoint but a sprawling realm.

The terse, catch-as-catch-can beauty of the poems in *Third Wish Wasted* depends upon a hurtling poetic line willing to risk apparent imprecision if that's what it takes to keep the language buzzing. It won't do to fuss pedantically about what exactly those "scimitar things" are, since this is a moment where, as in 'Your Sunday Best', "words lack mass", dropping back into what 'A Transatlantic Creed' describes as "belief in a voice [...] the shunting speed of sound". Such scepticism about straightforward perception prefigures the speaker of 'Keepsakes', left lying "in a wind-tossed dune", where I could never grow tanned

and no one could see your name tattooed
in ink the colour of skin
or the lock of hair snuck in my hand.

A characteristically punchy ending, as Lumsden's intuitive skill with rhyme and rhythm lets him stop on a dime to clinch his point. The title of the gorgeous 'Between the Penny Dropping and the Penny Landing' suggests the duration of his typical short lyric, and the poem itself describes the fine noise of time his best work lets us hear, "the half-chance sounding lower / than a cat-step or a spinning leaf or raindrops / meeting on a skylight".

David Constantine's *Nine Fathoms Deep* uses a similarly fast-moving line to evoke personal loss. 'The Woman in the House' gives us a husband's hands that have carried "The shock and quick of the sight of her / Almost without loss", and the syntax of 'The Mountains in the Mirror' is fast out of the blocks after a wry lead-in phrase: "it is clear", the poet writes,

> Without mercy what you are leaving and you know
> Those sharply in focus, framed, are only the few
> At the hub of a wheel of many more so that the sum
> Of loss you turn on is times and times of them.

Which isn't very clear at all. In his 'Prayer to the Ghosts', Constantine advises them to "speak clearly" and yet, like Lumsden's, his style responsibly acknowledges the difficulty of plain speaking. Such tangled writing as this remains connected, however, to the performative rhythms of a speaking voice trying to clear a space where life may proceed. To quote 'The Floor of the Ammonites': "In the small space between the sliding cliff and the sea / In the small time between the tides / Families come out from the little town to here".

Despite the historical reach suggested by the collection's notes, Constantine stays close, as ever, to the elements – the sea and the wind in particular. These Romantic images form the core of his imagination, and in 'Pity' he strikes a note of Wordsworthian affection for past paganism, for a "siren, a deep-sea triton or some such cross between" that might minister to a civilisation where:

> All's in the sights of the camera and the gun
> But we've no neighbourhood, no conversation.

As a strongly-worded ecological plea, the poem transcends the simplistic binary opposition between nature and culture which underwrites it.

Claire Crowther's second collection, *The Clockwork Gift*, subtly indulges and critiques an equally hoary connection between women and nature. 'The Herebefore' sensitively describes the poet's grandmother in her youth,

> [...] her lover lifting
>
> an empty crash of raw silk, a gorgeous
> light mass but she is aged by the sun
> far into rut and root. No one would know her.

Crowther writes with visual brilliance elsewhere of female ageing, describing in 'Woman, Probably One of the Fates' a wrinkled "inner arm" in terms of "Fate holding her drapery". The comparison with artworks and marble in that poem makes the point that women have traditionally been turned into objects to look at, and this is why their ageing is a taboo subject – unless it can be transformed into a symbol. Against such impositions, 'The Herebefore' re-asserts a natural continuity which gains its strength from the poet's questioning of her own artful procedures. By the time we reach the triumphant declaration at the end of the poem – "No skull but a new-coined queen" – elements of Heaney and his gendered bog poetry have started to show through, but they've been reclaimed and re-oriented.

Like Constantine, Crowther is less impressed with surfaces left relatively untextured by history; in 'Ubi Sunt', she comments of a former workplace that "its eery [*sic*] / insides deny I ever started there, /[...] deny that I worked my whole life behind glass." Such urban displacement echoes, mutedly, the more out-there despair of Sarah Wardle's *A Knowable World*, which returns repeatedly to an incident on a train which got the poet sectioned by the Sussex Police:

> they'll arrest you and drive you miles to a cell,
> where you'll be interviewed by a panel
> and the next morning carted off for a year in hospital.

This is the ending of 'Don't Try This Not At Home', a poem which sees the world as more disturbing and dangerous than knowable. Unsurprisingly given the circumstances, Wardle repeatedly writes constriction, either figurative or literal, as in 'Magnetic Resonance Imaging': "I kept speaking poems I had written / to myself, trapped inside that white coffin". Despite the injunction to the reader in 'Author! Author!' to "understand this print is not blood spilt on a page", her position remains essentially confessional: the several poems about the initial incident – 'Unnatural Justice', 'Flash', 'S 136' – make it clear that it all really happened, but printed together in one collection there's a sense of overkill about them. The most successful is 'Snow from Ebury Ward', whose beautiful, then jarring opening presents in microcosm the associative tendency of the book as a whole, describing snowflakes

> not settling, but hitting the ground to melt,
> like wasted hours, sectioned for losing one's mind.

Vidyan Ravinthiran is a graduate student and lecturer at Balliol College, Oxford. His pamphlet, *At Home or Nowhere*, was published by tall-lighthouse last year.

Fervour And Ironic Fervour

TIM LIARDET

Chris Wallace-Crabbe, *Telling a Hawk from a Handsaw*,
Carcanet, £9.95, ISBN 9781857549652;
Robert Minhinnick, *King Driftwood*, Carcanet, £9.95, ISBN 9781857549652

Chris Wallace-Crabbe is an altogether quieter, more thoughtful, craftier presence than Robert Minhinnick. In *Telling a Hawk from a Handsaw* there is fervour; but it is sophisticated, ironic. As a philosophical Australian poet, Wallace-Crabbe is at home in the company of Peter Porter, Les Murray and John Kinsella. If he is less of a civic poet than Porter, less a natural than Murray and less expansively energetic than Kinsella, he adds to such distinguished company the singing of the quotidian, a certain gift for idiosyncratic philosophy and what can only be termed a highly unusual, sometimes self-consciously Antipodean, diction, all beautifully combined in 'The Domestic Sublime':

who first spotted the lack
not that is the slip
in between the cup and lip
but down under a hot mug
or cup?
yet if it comes to that
a plate would merely be over the top [...]

On the one hand, Wallace-Crabbe explores a personal narrative without embellishment, can be movingly spare when striking emotional targets, and is particularly good at getting to grips with his father in poems which are refreshingly free of the kind of blame-laden and oedipal complexity that so often bedevils the father-son genre:

Father, you were able to praise
whatever I did, or had a shot at:
educationally creaky
but nourishing in the long-brisk haul,
you dear old bloke.   ('A Triptych for my Father')

The easy colloquy of this is one of his major hallmarks, I think, used to great effect over and over again. Combined with his raconteuring élan it produces moments of laid-back humour, as in 'Not Going to Korea After All': "Every morning, a little after sparrowfart / we shuffled onto the bullring / in boiler suit and blue cunt cap, / the flight sergeant wearily barking [...] in the pale dust of country roads / three of us broke the four minute mile: / the speedo must have been crook."

On the other hand, rather than submerge language he can embellish it too, and is happy at times to let his poetics become wholly visible: his language to be a proactive rather than a passive medium. Sometimes he is happy making short quasi-philosophical grasps, a simple idea decorated by its very ratiocination on the page; sometimes he simply allows his relish of language to rise to the surface, most beautifully in 'Ending with a Preposition': "Plenitude, the unseen flutefilled magpie / carolling its dulcet fanfaronade, / pleases us, drawing the past to guarantee /a separateness in every living thing."

As his poems get longer and his artistic universe grander, Robert Minhinnick proves he has made his peace with Dylan Thomas. For a male poet in Wales currently writing in English to be likened to perhaps the definitive Welsh poet can be considered a burden. Minhinnick carries it lightly, though:

the point of contact between the two is as much phonic as it is euphonic and this seems to be less the direct influence of Thomas, as such – a modelling on the part of Minhinnick – than the congruence of their backgrounds. They are of the same cultural blood-group. Both would argue, I suspect, that poetry is a force-field existing primarily in sound.

The fourteenth section of 'An Opera in Baghdad' opens with lines in which Minhinnick proves he can out-Thomas Thomas:

> The bird in its cage sang an ancient maqam
> of flowering fountains and rivers that ran,
> of the rivers of Babylon, gentle to man.

Rhythmically, phonetically, this juggles similar notes to those at large in Thomas's 'Altarwise by Owl-light,' say, or 'Our Eunuch Dreams' or 'This Bread I Break'. Beyond the sounds, however, Minhinnick, like Thomas, knows that for language to be a vital force it must be allowed to break the surface of the poem rather than merely servicing it. It must also be rapturous, it must woo rapture; inversions and the mixing of the demotic with the urbane are therefore very much the point. Perhaps above all, so is repetition. Minhinnick writes in the seventh section of 'An Opera in Baghdad:' "The Tigris and the Thames. The Tigris and the Thames. / The Tigris black with blood. / The Thames all black with blood". There's not much irony in Minhinnick, but plenty of instinct.

Here the similarities end. If Thomas inhabited world as much imagined as idealised, there is no doubting that Minhinnick is out there in the destructive reality of Two-Thousand-and-Nine. War, famine, global warming and the many daily injustices of the world are his essential nutrients. He is now one of the most overtly political poets currently writing in the UK. This results in unlikely imagistic bed-follows and a preparedness to take risks which is at times, frankly, jaw-dropping:

> Two wrens had made a nest in his fist
> and money spider spun their moss
> in a crease of Joseph Stalin's coat,
> Uncle Joe whose proletarian
> ferro-concrete pointed at the falling leaves
> of a birch whose bark was a burnt missal [...] ('An Isotope, Dreaming')

King Driftwood is a book of huge ambition: of one hundred and thirty pages, on the one hand, only twenty six poems on the other. These figures suggest poems which are extending themselves symphonically (two are ten pages long) and whose focus is deepening. If at the core of his poetics there is a poet's authentic relationship with the world, Minhinnick is always in the mix himself, exploring his own congress with the experience in hand.

Tim Liardet is Professor of Creative Writing at Bath Spa University. His collection *The Blood Choir* (2006) was shortlisted for the T.S.Eliot Prize.

Growth-Rings In Poems

DAVID MORLEY

Esther Jansma, *What It Is: Selected Poems*, trans. Francis R Jones, Bloodaxe, £8.95, ISBN 9781852247805; *Lament for the Wanderer*, trans. Jane Holland, Heaventree Press, £4, ISBN 9781906038069; Daniel Samoilovich, *Driven by the Wind and Drenched to the Bone*, trans. Andrew Graham-Yooll, Shoestring Press, £8.95, ISBN 9781904886600; Yi Sha, *Starve the Poets! Selected Poems*, trans. Simon Patton and Tao Naikan, Bloodaxe, £9.95, ISBN 9781852248154; Mourid Barghouti, *Midnight and Other Poems*, trans. Radwa Ashour, Arc Publications, £14.39, ISBN 9781906570088; *Flowers of Flame: Unheard Voices of Iraq*, ed. Sadek Mohammed, Soheil Najm, Haider Al_Kabi, and Dan Veach, Michigan State University Press, £14.50, ISBN 9780870138423; Vítzslav Nezval, *Prague with Fingers of Rain*, trans. Ewald Osers, Bloodaxe, £8.95, ISBN 9781852248161

Antonio Machado claimed that, "In order to write poetry, you must first invent a poet who will write it". It might be a smart move to invent your translator while you're at it. Robert Frost's over-celebrated remark that "Poetry is what is lost in translation" may make poets of other languages feel unattainable, but what Frost went on to say was, "It is also what is lost in interpretation", which makes attainability a little problematic. And it says more about the nature of poetry than it does about the process of translation, or of criticism for that matter. Few enough writers realise that good translation, like good criticism, is a vocation and its practice as thorny as original composition. Translation is always a negotiation which, to paraphrase Ngugi wa Thiong'o, moves beyond and around language.

Some words are charged with particular meanings in the original language; that does not ensure those associations in another tongue.

It is not only the spectrum of meaning that is considered in excellent poetic translation. There are polyphonies of factors: the physical sound of the poem's internal movement; the speed, shiver and intent of word-notes, taken individually, within a line, and within a whole poem. And what about the meanings of the sounds of words, the tongues and voices ringing and ringed in the grain of poetic lines, and the notion of locality in how a word is spoken and understood? The Dutch poet and archaeologist Esther Jansma, who established the age of wooden artefacts from growth-ring, might show us whether there are growth-rings in a poem's language and form. Her translator writes, in the introduction to the excellent *What It Is*, that "if a source poem is rhymed, some translators see the rhyme as somehow 'separate from' meaning [...] I feel that if rhyme is used, it is part of a poem's meaning". Author and translator held a painstaking negotiation over every draft, and their teamwork makes for a convincing, clear, almost scientifically-eyed poetry:

> If we have to dress, when all is said at last
> against the cold or in something's name
> in what remains of this or another past
> tales and aides-memoire which simply claim
>
> that we were here and nothing more
> in time which existed before today [...]   ('Archaeology 2')

With the exception of Jane Holland's persuasive and energetic version of *The Wanderer*, the books under review here are all 'beyond and around' translation, in that they are neither re-imaginings nor imitations. Of Holland's delightful appropriation of the Anglo-Saxon original, she states that "the switch from Christian to secular beliefs and the switch from male to female narrator were acts of reinterpretation [...] Those who find this change too much of a strain [...] should consider that each age must reinvent the classics rather than simply 'translate' them [...]". She is correct of course: except there is nothing simple about translation, which decides the posterity of certain poems. For example, *Driven by the Wind and Drenched to the Bone* by the Argentinian Daniel Samoilovich is a beautifully selected collection of sharp, startling, colourful lyrical poems. Shoestring Press has done admirably to bring this fine poet to attention in the UK. This small selection of translations reveals a poetry that is nettled by the history of the author's country, but nettled into fastidious and gorgeous perception. His translator has showed him to advantage. Conversely, I got the underwhelming feeling in *Starve the Poets!* that the selection of work from "controversial Chinese poet" Yi Sha shows him to full disadvantage. The translators have done almost too good a job in rendering into English what seems to me a self-regarding, self-important, sexist set of work. It's almost as if Yi Sha had taken the least attractive tonal elements of Bukowski then done his best to divest his poetry of the quality of mercy. The trouble is that we passed through this phase some time ago: half-pretending to enjoy poems that yielded the reader zero except the corrosion of attention. Eye-wateringly, this appears to be one of the stated intentions of the author; except he believes he's being laconic rather than tedious:

> Walking across life's stage.
>
> Just now
> as I handed him a cigarette
> he gave me a light
>
> Walking across life's stage
>
> In the flickering flames
> I got a glimpse of his cigarette lighter –
> well, what d'you know?: it was shaped like a mini-
> fire extinguisher.   ('Crossing the Stage')

Some poets argue that all writing is translated from silence. *Midnight and Other Poems* by the Palestinian writer Mourid Barghouti reads like a series of skilful resurrections, through language, of a silenced majority:

> After the dust and smoke
> have cleared from the house that once stood there
> and as I stare at the new emptiness,
> I see my grandfather wearing his cloak,
> wearing the very same cloak –
> not one similar to it,
> but the same one.
> He hugs me and maintains a silent gaze,
> as if his look
> could order the rubble to become a house [...]   ('Midnight')

'Midnight' is an ambitious sequence, a montage of images from the land of Barghouti's birth, and rewards being read aloud. One gets the feeling it is written to be heard, and can be considered part of a wider debate about language, land and dispossession, rather like the interesting poems in *Flowers of Flame*, by new poets of Iraq.

I move, finally, to the resonant and gloriously complex *Prague with Fingers of Rain* by Czech writer Vítizslav Nezval, first published in 1936, and translated here by the brilliant Ewald Osers. This is an expert evocation of Prague's interwar liveliness and polyvalence. What's especially exciting is how landscape and streetscape are rendered clearly and precisely within an apparently 'surrealist' confection of forms and strategies. We are only just catching up with such approaches. It is unlikely you will have read anything else quite like this collection, not only in terms of meaning and structure, but also ricocheting forms and acutely-judged sound.

David Morley is Professor of Creative Writing at the University of Warwick.

The Beauty Of Home

SARAH MASKILL

Peter Bennet, *The Glass Swarm*, Flambard, £7.50, ISBN 9781873226995;
Sarah Corbett, *Other Beasts*, Seren, £7.99, ISBN 9781854114662;
Todd Swift, *Seaway; New and Selected Poems*, Salmon, €15.00,
ISBN 9781903392928;
Jane Holland, *Camper Van Blues*, Salt, £12.99, ISBN 9781844714674

"We might be anywhere but are in one place only." Bennet quotes Derek Mahon in his poem 'The Ballroom at Blaxter Hall', where the ballroom is still furnished with the apparatus of courtship but abandoned and cobwebbed. Portraying what was a grand home, where comfort has been replaced by a "catafalque" and the chandelier becomes "wasps' nest", Bennet charts the fortunes of this "home of lost romance" and those of its inhabitants, weaving Northumberland into a collection steeped in timeless, placeless folklore.

In 'Greta', the march of progress has devalued the estate and made it less family home and more disposable. Gertrude speaks of "this wilderness of useless moor / to which I'll bring a squad of men and lorries / with steel and glass to build the new aesthetic". However, she concludes:

> there's a shimmer on the mossy gravel
> like thought becoming crystalline
> beside the Seine, the Spree, the Tyne.

This deft siting of the universal within the local is attributable to Bennet's accomplished knitting-together of thematic and balladic elements. Bennet also explores commonality: 'St George's Day' celebrates the "[...] the people – / who danced today and work the land in common". Their hands are "our hands, but with callouses." Parity before death in 'Danse Macabre' is coupled with nightmarish visions generating a malaise that pervades the collection. Unattainable desire is another motif. 'The Lens' neatly shows three aims – taking a photograph, having children, smashing a window – which all fail. The pursuit of something meant to bring personal peace is a source of unrest, and these poems effectively convey that disquiet.

Concerned with location and also the beginnings of creative identity, Corbett explores both in her prose poem, 'My Border Ancestry': "I learnt to whistle in the woods at Ewloe, my hand in my father's hand, the sound coming at first [...] more spit than song." Identity is forged in 'Breaking Horses', where there is no choice but to face scenes of cruelty:

> the small boy Raskolnikov holding
> all that time his mother's hand,
> this one anchor tying him to the horror,
> pushing it back somewhere –

These are momentous episodes, and the poet describes being "sent skittering on / like a yearling with its rump slapped." Her geography is instinctual rather than map-read. In 'Taking the Night Train, "I [...] felt the unseen // bodies of mountains press out the dawn", and in 'Rainbow':

> In the hotel room we saw the beauty of home,
> too far out to touch still, and effervescently moving.

Mixing beauty and trauma, Corbett's verse is also cinematic. 'Testimony' describes how "Things came back, not my whole / life but scenes [...] a pile of edits / together". 'Cuttings' comprises flickering news pieces that juxtapose killings, cruelty and art. Yet, 'Seen From Above' gives us an "earth [...] seen from space, / the whole fluent marble of her" – a quiet, photographic icon, reminding us that such disquiets are, all the while, part of a peaceful whole.

Todd Swift's new poems often flaunt self-conscious poetics. 'Form and the Line', an articulate villanelle, is itself like the "church made to shape a sound that prays". 'One Hundred Lines' associates writing with traditional school punishment: again, the idea of hardship is associated with aesthetics. 'Early Work' explores the development of poetic expression from youth, where "Language sobbed", to the mature assertion that "Most feeling's preordained". As Swift's collection bundles old and new offerings, it's possible to observe the reassessment of identity and origin being carried out within it. An early poem of disconnection, 'Kanada Post' remembers "some other life as if it's mine" and how "It's not a country if it only happens when it's gone". The more recent 'The Red Bathing Cap' is poised and memorable, and the sentiments have undergone a sea-change. The poet's mother is in focus: "You swam out // Clean and strong" and "Beautiful, tall". As she swims, the narrator reads "*Mimesis* / Or some anthology", amalgamating the remembering poet and the remembering son. The assertion that "You're older – water / Cannot keep us young // Forever" suggests unwelcome wisdom and precedes the stark concluding image:

> Red cap – (brightened like
> A pricked thumb) –
>
> [...] a sewing
> Needle, threading water
> With your breathing stroke –
> Is like a light, a light to me.

Swift presents the concept of home as a final destination, a place of comfort, as well as a fulfilment of familial obligation:

> the where and why
> Of home, of coming home.
> I'll bring your blue towel.

Holland's poems map the aftermath of personal calamity and consequent attempts at defragmentation. Self-imposed exile is a form of self-harm as she recounts life at motorway lay-bys and the wheel of her mobile home. Self-punishment alternates with moments of strength. 'Neighbours' portrays someone almost at ease with circumstances as she "swings through from the cab / to table", yet in 'Bone Flute':

> Now I've travelled this far, worn to the stub
>   forgetting you,
>
> I'm a bone flute
>   for the wind to whistle through [...]

There are also moments of pure glee. In 'Giants of the Motorway' the narrator becomes a dignified "white queen of the road". 'In Praise of Speed' sees poet become petrolhead, fraternising with the hostile world of the road as her "soul sings / selfishly / for speed – the wild, instinctual / thrust of it".

This poetry borrows from older literature, and the yearning to return – perhaps not to home, but to a time or consciousness before hardship – makes a path through the third part of this volume. Superstitions and folklore suggest the fragility of human existence and vain attempts to hang on to it. 'Rain' imagines "the beginning of things", and 'St John's Chapel' the vanishing "[...] back into green." So Holland's poetry of travel, a resettlement without settling in the margins of society, is a resonant lament for the broken promises of ideals, and for the elusiveness of peace.

Sarah Maskill studied creative writing at University of St Andrews.

ENDPAPERS

Topping up... the bubble wand on the tomb of the unknown writer.

– *Peter Blegvad*

LETTER FROM REYKJAVÍK

ROBIN VAUGHAN-WILLIAMS

In 1985 Marshall Brement, an American diplomat and translator posted in Iceland, enthused about Iceland as a place "where poetry is an every-day commodity, where poets are national heroes". In doing so he echoed the sentiments of W.H.Auden who, almost fifty years earlier, had written: "what struck me most is that any average educated person one meets can turn out competent verse".

When Auden visited Iceland in 1936, modernism had yet to take root. Formal experimentation was liable to be villified on the right as 'degenerate' and on the left as 'decadent'. The country had only gained independence from Denmark in 1918, and Iceland's unique literary heritage, the fact that *sagas* and *eddas* (epic poems), written in the thirteenth and fourteenth centuries were still comprehensible to modern Icelanders, played an important role in the nationalist movement. For a while, abandoning the traditional forms and subjects of Icelandic verse must have seemed contrary to the national mood, and to risk alienation from the popular readership. The purist language policy, which aims to protect Icelandic from foreign (and dialectical) influence, is something the more experimental poets struggle with even today.

So was Marshall Brement right, were poets in the late twentieth century still "national heroes", or was he referring to poets of the past? From the Atom Poets of the 1950s, most poetry in Iceland has been distinctively modern (or post-modern), but this did not stop the Bad Great Poets (*Listaskáldin vondu*) performing to over 1,000 people at Reykjavík's University Cinema in 1976, and in 2008 over a hundred books of poetry were published in Iceland (equivalent to about 21,000 in the UK).

Nevertheless, there is a widespread feeling of marginalisation among Icelandic poets, who have had to cope with recurring discussions about the 'death of poetry'. Maybe the death of the poet is really a reference to "modern multitasking", ponders the (very much alive) poet Sigurbjörg Þrastardóttir, since most people who write poems "also do novels, visual arts, theatre and what not". This engagement in multiple art forms is indeed prevalent among contemporary Icelandic poets, and is perhaps itself a strategy for dealing with the relatively diminutive status of poetry. "Poetry", Eiríkur Norðdahl explains, "is very much seen as a hobby [...] It's a training ground, you hone your wordskills in poetry, then turn to prose when your muscles are up to it."

The struggle against marginalisation could be seen as a common thread running through successive generations of modern Icelandic poets. The Bad Great Poets employed pop-cultural references and sought to de-auratise poetry, after the minimalist purism of their predecessors. One of their members, Þórarinn Eldjarn, is renowned for his *Disney Rhymes* (*Disneyrímur*, 1978), in which he re-tells the story of Walt Disney using the epic *rímur* form. In the 1980s the surrealist group Medúsa combined poetry with other art forms in multimedia performances, and allied itself with the rather anti-heroic punk scene.

More recently, in 2003, the artgroup Nýhil took a travelling circus of poets and artists around Iceland in order to reach out beyond the boundaries of Reykjavík. By publishing, polemicising, translating, organising international poetry festivals, and providing a public forum, Nýhil (lit. 'new-hilism') has contributed to a renewed sense of excitement about poetry in Iceland. Members of the group range from the lyrical poet Kristín Eiríksdóttir to Eiríkur Norðdahl, one of its founders, who is influenced by the avant-garde tradition of sound poetry and the impulse to 'make over' the language. Interesting work is also being produced by plenty of unaffiliated poets, such as Sigurbjörg Þrastardóttir, Kristín Ómarsdóttir, and Sölvi Björn Sigurðsson, whose *Diabolical Comedy* (2005) faithfully renders a drunken binge through Reykjavík in Dantean terzinas.

Robin Vaughan-Williams recently moved to Iceland from Sheffield, where he ran 'Spoken Words Antics'.

The National Poetry Competition

*P*oetry Review is glad to continue our annual tradition of publishing the wining poems from the National Poetry Competition. This year, the judges were Frieda Hughes, Jack Mapanje and Brian Patten. Of the winner, Patten says, "[...] one of the marks of a good poet is the ability to turn the private into the universal, and that is what Christopher does in this affectionate poem."

FIRST PRIZE

Christopher James
Farewell To The Earth

We buried him with a potato in each hand
on New Year's Day when the ground was hard as luck,
wearing just cotton, his dancing shoes plus
a half bottle of pear cider to stave off the thirst.

In his breast pocket we left a taxi number
and a packet of sunflower seeds; at his feet was
the cricket bat he used to notch up a century
against the Fenstanton eleven.

We dropped in his trowel and a shower of rosettes
then let the lid fall on his willow casket.
The sky was hard as enamel; there was
a callus of frost on the face of the fields.

Dust to dust; but this was no ordinary muck.
The burial plot was by his allotment, where
the water butt brimmed with algae and the shed door
swung and slammed as we shook back the soil.

During the service, my mother asked
the funeral director to leave; take away some hair
and the resemblance was too close; and yet
my father never looked so smart.

I kept expecting him to walk in, his brow
steaming with rain, soil under his fingernails
smelling of hot ashes and compost;
looking for fresh tea in the pot.

SECOND PRIZE

Charles Evans
Libretto

The heroine lay dying in her pasteboard cot
Seized by coughing, clutching with both hands
The big tenor who knelt at her side
It was too much
I slipped from my seat, stumbled through feet and knees
Mounted the stage in a burst of saving love
For heaven's sake, I said, *she's a sick woman*
An attic is no place for a consumptive
They hustled me to the wings

She took the stage, flaunting her gypsy skirt
In a fast spin, taunting with jutting hips
The workers who crowded close
I saw the danger
Hurried down, pushed aside the protesting musicians
Climbed the steps in a last bid to stop the brawl
Calm down, I told them, *love's all right in its place*
But there's no need for knives
They escorted me to the foyer

He reached out, touching the breasts of the peasant girl
In a sly gesture, reassuring her
He was a rich man, her key to a new life
I was disgusted
Stood up, decided to give him a piece of my mind
Burst out in a last attempt to protect her virtue
Come off it, I shouted, *we all know what you want*
Take your hands off that poor girl
They marched me to the door

Outside, I saw the bus, splashed through driving rain
Slipped in a puddle, fell heavily on the oily road
Under the big Jag, which screeched to a halt
I gathered my senses
Sat up, heard the chorus of concern
Broke into song in an effort to find the key
Take it easy, they said, *the ambulance is here*
This is no time for singing
They cut short my aria

THIRD PRIZE

Clive McWilliam
Holding On

My tiny aunt was always afraid
she might be blown away. She fluttered about
in the draft of her house chasing snails
that slid under the door. Each night she climbed
a steepening stair to lie beneath the stars'
straining light, hidden in sodium glare.

Her four room cave in the shade of passing
buses, where daylight goes
to snooze, with two knotted dollies
standing guard in a chair
and a wardrobe of tiny shoes.

You must have left the door ajar
the night the snails brought you the light
of stars on their backs, for the wind got in
and swept your house and blew you clean away.

LETTER TO THE EDITOR*

We note that the review section of the latest edition of *Poetry Review* is entirely divided along gender lines: six men poets are reviewed by four male critics, while seven women poets are reviewed by three female critics.[I] This is not the first time this has occurred recently: in Summer 2008, twenty-one collections by women were reviewed by women, and twenty-one collections by men reviewed by men,[II] while the issue of Spring 2008 grouped all its poets in the same way.[III] In fact, of your last forty-five reviews of more than one collection, only ten have mixed women poets with men poets.

The impression given is that poetry by women is separate from men's poetry. Distribution of space within the magazine also suggests that it is less important: in the last six issues, men have enjoyed eight prominent solo reviews, but women only four, while nineteen men poets have been reviewed in pairs as against nine women.[IV] On the other hand, the last six issues offer ten 'women's round-ups' in which groups of three or more women poets are reviewed by another woman, under titles such as 'Feminine Diction' (Summer 2008) and '...what women poets share' (Winter 2008).[V] This creates the idea that a woman poet's theme is always her gender, and that women are writing for, and can only be read by, each other. For example, in the 'Green Issue', Jean Sprackland's 'Tilt' was reviewed with three other women poets under the title 'celebrating the liveliness of women writers'.[VI] 'Tilt' was thus implicitly excluded from the surrounding ecological debate, though the collection is powerfully concerned with green themes. No grouping of men in the magazine has ever been given a title, or a critique, which considers their masculinity; though gender is surely a theme for both sexes.

Women critics are correspondingly diminished: only four women have written solo reviews in your last six issues, while eight men have done so; three women have been given paired, reviews, while nine went to men.[VII] Nor are women essayists and thinkers valued: twenty-two Centrefold pieces in the last six issues have been authored by men, but only four by women. Poems by women are fewer than poems by men too: in fact, of 721 pages of articles, poems, reviews and editorials in the last six issues, only 201 have been filled by women writers, or about twenty eight per cent.[VIII] We do not believe that women are twenty eight per cent of Poetry, and we do not believe you think so either. *Poetry Review* is important to us: it is a central magazine which sets the tone for other publications, and which may very well supply

---

*Inaccuracies in the figures given here are noted below on p. 124.

the poems and collections, on which we work so hard, with their audience and with their sole or definitive reading. It is also one of the very few places where a new critic or essayist may develop. At present, *Poetry Review* is not allowing us that space as critics and is ghettoising and diminishing our work as poets because of our gender. Poetry and women has an unequal and vexed history: we do not expect this to be abolished, but we do think it should be addressed. We hope that more will be done in the future to give women poets a balanced reading, and allow women critics and thinkers a share of the debate.

Kate Clanchy, Patience Agbabi, Kate Kingham, Polly Clark, Julia Copus, Claire Crowther, Carrie Etter, Annie Freud, Carola Luther, Katrina Porteous, Anne Rouse, Eva Salzman, Greta Stoddart and Susan Wicks

Presumably the signatories to this letter don't mean that women should be published on a quota basis. *PR* publishes women (and men) because they are fine poets and critics.

Actual experience of editing teaches that it is indeed a creative but also *de facto* a reflective role. Women are taking their rightful places at the top table, among the most important and acknowledged poets in Britain. Nevertheless, ours remains an asymmetric profession, and the *Review* cannot correct this either overnight or, indeed, single-handedly. It can, however, advocate poetry purely on its *textual* merits, whatever the writer's gender, orientation, class or cultural or ethnic background; and whether s/he is well-established or a newcomer.

PR practices further transparency in balancing a range of poetics. It commissions the best reviewer for each piece: where "best" is taken to mean "having some understanding of these poetics", *not* "a personal friend of" and *not* "likely to give good copy by savaging". As readers will have noticed, *PR* dispenses with both the log-rolling and the Rottweiler review, instead grouping collections in ways which secure them a fair reading. As with anthologists (including, recently, Salzman and Wack), or academic specialists, it is still surprisingly often the case that the accurate reader with most understanding of women's poetics is a woman herself. She may indeed allude to gender issues: since, as the above letter demonstrates, they remain peculiarly problematised for women's writing.

Though some of the figures given in this letter are not only inaccurate (see 'A note on the figures') but tendentious – for example, they count-in the over-whelmingly masculine Porter tribute, which appeared toward the end of the weeks during which it was circulating in search of signatures – the writers do hit upon a central truth about British poetry. The number of participants, at every level from prizes and editorships to (it transpires) established poets who send their work into magazines, are strikingly unequal. In particular, there are very few women critics. Over-represented among literature administrators, women seem disproportionately reluctant to assume literary authority through regular reviewing – leave alone essay-writing – though there are of course fine exceptions who prove the rule. This is not to suggest that our senior women poets have time on their hands: many have moved with distinction into anthologising, writing memoir and fiction, and teaching. But it's terrific news, in terms of a spread of role models, that we also have new women poetry editors at *Poetry Wales* and *Poetry London*.

Editing is multi-form: paramount, for the feminist, is never to sacrifice even one woman's writing – poetry or criticism – for personal political gain. Gender studies, at least as this editor has taught them over the years, show us the other side of agency is responsibility. Today's pre-eminent (women) poets remind us just how much is achieved by seriousness, excellence – and, of course, participation.

A note on the figures
I. In fact, the 7 women are reviewed by two women and a man (Alex Smith). An 8th woman, the Geoffrey Dearmer winner, is reviewed by Peter Porter. **II.** 22 books by women are reviewed; the issue includes a mixed-gender-group review. **III.** Of its 9 reviewers 6 are women, who include 2 (Hilary Barker and Alice Kavounas) reviewing men. **IV.** 8 reviews pair books by men, 4 pair M/F and 3 pair F. **V.** Of group reviews of 3 or more poets, the numbers are: all-women poets – 11, all-men – 9, mixed-gender – 10. Some sample titles of all-women reviews: 'Satire and sensibility', 'Darkness and Light', 'What our Bones Know'. **VI.** The title was 'Green Shoots'. **VII.** Reviewers of paired collections are M – 10 F – 5. **VIII.** Of 731 contributor pages, 281, or 40%, are written by or about women. – Ed.

CONTRIBUTORS

Timothy Allen won a 2008 Stephen Spender Prize for the opening of *A New Lament for a Broken Heart;* **Elizabeth Barrett**'s *The Bat Detector* appears from Wrecking Ball Press and Meridien Records; **Arthur Boyars** edited *Mandrake* (1946-58) and appeared in *The New Poetry* (ed. Alvarez, 1962); **Fred Beake**'s *New and Selected Poems* appears from Shearsman; **Margo Berdeshevsky**'s *But a Passage in Wilderness* is published by Sheep Meadow Press; **Dejan Bogojevic** is an artist, publisher and widely-translated poet; **Wojciech Bonowicz** has published six collections, awards include the Gdynia Prize; **Dan Burt**'s pamphlet is *Searched for Text;* his first collection is forthcoming from Carcanet; **Peter Carpenter**'s *After the Goldrush,* (Nine Arches Press) is due this autumn; **Wendy Cope**'s most recent book is *Two Cures for Love: selected poems 1979-2006;* **Patrick Dubost** has published more than twenty collections (including under the alias Armand Le Poête) and several CDs; **Tadeusz Dąbrowski** is a poet and literary editor, awards include the "Small Sceptre", Polish Cultural Foundation; **Tsvetanka Elenkova** is widely translated; **Menna Elfyn** is one of the leading Welsh-language poets; **Sean Elliott**'s pamphlet is *Waterhouse and the Tempest* (Acumen, 2009); **Ruth Fainlight**'s *Collected Poems* appears next year. Her poems in Spanish translation are just published by Cosmopoética; **Atar Hadari**'s *Songs from Bialik* (Syracuse University Press 2000) was short-listed for the American Literary Translator's Association Award; **A.A.Marcoff** is an Anglo-Russian poet who has lived in Africa, Iran, France and Japan; **Daljit Nagra**'s *Look We Have Coming to Dover* won the Forward First Book Prize; **D Nurkse** has received the Whiting Writers Award and two NEA fellowships; **Luko Paljetak** is an award-winning Croatian poet; **Pascale Petit**'s latest collection is *The Treekeeper's Tale* (Seren, 2008). She has been twice shortlisted for the T.S.Eliot Prize; **Alexandar Prokopiev**'s *Peeper* was shortlisted for the 2008 Balkan Prize; **Primoz Repar** has published nine collections of poetry and of essays; **Omar Sabbagh**'s *My Only Ever Oedipal Complaint* is forthcoming (2010, Cinnamon Press); **Jo Shapcott** has published fifteen books to date, her many prizes include the Forward Prize and a Cholmondeley Award; **Penelope Shuttle** lives in Cornwall. Her ninth collection, *The Repose of Baghdad*, appears next year. ; **Julian Stannard**'s latest book is *The Red Zone* (Peterloo, 2007); **Janet Sutherland**'s second collection *Hangman's Acre* (Shearsman Books) will be published in October 2009; **Kay Syrad**'s most recent publication is *Objects of Colour: Baltic Coast;* **Siriol Troup**'s second collection, *Beneath the Rime*, is published by Shearsman; **Fred Voss** is an American poet; **John Whitworth**'s 'Religion and Poetry' appeared in *PR* 98:4; **Susan Wicks**'s most recent collection is *De-iced* (2007).

Dorothy Sargent Rosenberg Annual Poetry Prizes, 2009

PRIZE WINNERS FOR OUR 2008 COMPETITION, ANNOUNCED 5 FEBRUARY 2009

$7500 PRIZES to Elizabeth Adams, Katy Didden and Melissa Mylchreest

$5,000 PRIZES to Matthew James Babcock , Brian Brodeur, Tom Christopher, Temple Cone, Julie Dunlop, Brieghan Gardner, Jules Gibbs, Garth Greenwell, Emily Ruth Hazel, Ann Hudson, Melissa Stein, Natalia Trevino, Rhett Iseman Trull and Laura Van Prooyen

$2,500 PRIZES to Paula Bohince, Gillian Cummings, Rachel Dilworth, Melina Draper, Robin Ekiss, Patrick Foran, Rae Gouirand, Megan Gravendyk , Katherine Anne Hays, Elizabeth Kay, Bethany Tyler Lee, Debbie Lim, Melissa Mack, Christopher Nelson, Alison Pelegrin, Anna Lena Phillips, Brian Spears, Tess Taylor, Emily Tuszynska and Jacqueline West

$1000 PRIZES to Allyson Arndt, Michele Battiste, Michael Boccardo, Brian Brown, Samantha Buchanan, Melisa Cahnmann Taylor, Chuck Carlise, Caitlin Doyle, Jacqueline Gabbitas, Marie Gauthier, Julia Guez, Valerie Linet , Cath Nichols, Gregory W. Randall, Chad Sweeney, Nicole Foreman Tong and Benjamin Vogt

There were also thirteen Honorable Mentions at $250 each

THANK YOU TO EVERYONE WHO ENTERED AND CONGRATULATIONS TO OUR WINNERS

WE NOW HAPPILY ANNOUNCE OUR

2009 Competition

Prizes ranging from $1,000 up to as much as $25,000 will be awarded for the finest lyric poems celebrating the human spirit. The contest is open to all writers, published or unpublished, who will be under the age of 40 years on 6 November 2009. Entries must be postmarked on or before the third Saturday in October (17 October 2009). Only previously unpublished poems are eligible for prizes. Names of prize winners will be published on our website on 5 February 2010, together with a selection of the winning poems. Please visit our website www.DorothyPrizes.org for further information and to read poems by previous winners.

CHECKLIST OF CONTEST GUIDELINES
- Entries must be postmarked on or before 17 October 2009.
- Past winners may re-enter until their prizes total in excess of $25,000.
- All entrants must be under the age of 40 on November 6, 2009.
- Submissions must be original, previously unpublished, and in English: no translations, please.
- Each entrant may submit one to three separate poems.
- Only one of the poems may be more than thirty lines in length.
- Each poem must be printed on a separate sheet.
- Submit two copies of each entry with your name, address, phone number and email address clearly marked on each page of one copy only.
- Include an index card with your name, address, phone number and email address and the titles of each of your submitted poems.
- Include a $10 entry fee payable to the Dorothy Sargent Rosenberg Memorial Fund. (Not required for entries mailed from outside U.S.A.)
- Poems will not be returned. Include a stamped addressed envelope if you wish us to acknowledge receipt of your entry.

MAIL ENTRIES TO: Dorothy Sargent Rosenberg Poetry Prizes, PO Box 2306, Orinda, California 94563, USA

POOR. OLD. TIRED. HORSE.

17 JUNE—23 AUGUST 2009
INSTITUTE OF CONTEMPORARY ARTS
LONDON

An exhibition on art
and poetry, featuring:

Vito Acconci
Carl Andre
Anna Barham
Matthew Brannon
Henri Chopin
Ian Hamilton Finlay
Alasdair Gray
Philip Guston
David Hockney
Karl Holmqvist
Dom Sylvester Houédard
Janice Kerbel
Christopher Knowles
Ferdinand Kriwet
Liliane Lijn
Robert Smithson
Frances Stark
Sue Tompkins

www.ica.org.uk/pooroldtiredhorse

ARTS COUNCIL
ENGLAND

Image: Liliane Lijn, *Sky Never Stops*, 1965, Collection V&A Museum, London

MA Creative Writing:

Novel, Poetry and Writing for Children at the Writing School, Manchester Metropolitan University

Under the direction of Poet Laureate Carol Ann Duffy, MMU's Writing School is a thriving centre of creative excellence offering a suite of ambitious degree programmes delivered by distinguished practising writers.

Follow the Novel or Poetry routes full time (two years) or part time (three years) or the Writing for Children route part time (three years). The Novel and Poetry routes are also available to study online (three years).

Tutors include: Simon Armitage, Sherry Ashworth, Heather Beck, Vicki Bertram, Andrew Biswell, Carol Ann Duffy, Paul Magrs, Jennifer Mayhew, Jacqueline Roy, Nicholas Royle, Michael Symmons Roberts and Jean Sprackland.

The MA programme includes the following elements:

Workshop: develop your creative and editorial skills under the guidance of an established practitioner.

Literature Courses: focus on formal and stylistic aspects of outstanding contemporary writing.

The Text: learn about the state of the publishing industry with visits from expert speakers and guest authors.

Transmission Project: devise an independent research project specific to your skills and interests.

Portfolio: guided by a published author, produce a completed book, presented to professional standard.

The Writing School also offers a range of accredited **Continuing Professional Development courses** for teachers and writers interested in teaching creative writing in school or community settings. There is also an optional unit in Literary Translation.

For an application pack, please call +44 (0) 161 247 6969 or email courses@mmu.ac.uk

For further information, contact James Draper on +44 (0) 161 247 1787 or j.draper@mmu.ac.uk, or go to: www.hlss.mmu.ac.uk/english/writingschool

www.hlss.mmu.ac.uk/english/writingschool
The University for World-Class Professionals